Season

Philippians 4:13

Lou White

Growing Season

Lori White

TATE PUBLISHING
AND ENTERPRISES, LLC

Published by Tate Publishing & Enterprises, LLC
127 E. Trade Center Terrace | Mustang, Oklahoma 73064 USA
1.888.361.9473 | www.tatepublishing.com

Tate Publishing is committed to excellence in the publishing industry. The company reflects the philosophy established by the founders, based on Psalm 68:11,
"The Lord gave the word and great was the company of those who published it."

Published in the United States of America

ISBN: 978-1-68118-250-6
1. Biography & Autobiography / Personal Memoirs
2. Religion / Christian Life / Inspirational
15.03.26

Preface

August 8 marks the only logical day for me to start writing this book. August 8 marks my dear grandmother's birthday. It marks the day my dad passed away. Yes, August 8 is a significant day. It is also the day my growing season began.

When I think of seasons, I typically think of the four seasons that we celebrate each year in northwest Iowa. My favorite author, Karen Kingsbury, talks a lot about seasons of life in her books. Some seasons last longer than others.

August 8, 2009, my growing season began. I wait and wonder, how long will this growing season last? Trials are enduring and seeing an end in sight is encouraging. A farmer plants his crops and waits patiently during growing season, waiting for harvest. This growing season lasts a few months.

Today, the day I start writing it all down, marks the two-year anniversary of my growing season. There are days when I am past ready for harvest. There are other days when I can only hope that my growing season will continue for the rest of my life.

I am choosing to share my experiences for several reasons. Writing has always been a passion of mine and very therapeutic for me. The last two years have been hard, and it is time for healing. But my main reason for writing this book is because I believe it could help others. My prayer is that someone will pick up this book and gain some encouragement that everything will be okay if you keep your focus on God. That is really what my growing season is about, learning to keep my focus on God.

CHAPTER 1

Growing Pains

August 8, 2009. For the last several months I had been working as a committee member preparing for our county's Relay for Life. This is an annual event for our county and my first year as cochair. The last few months have been hectic. In July, I was notified that I had been blessed with a job. This was to be my first full-time teaching job. I was excited to begin. First things first, though. I was committed to Relay.

For those who don't know, Relay for Life is an annual event that takes place all over the country. Local volunteers set up the overnight walk along with speakers, entertainment, and booths with games and food to raise money for the American Cancer Society. This is a cause that is near and dear to my heart. August 8, 2009, not only marked the Relay, but also marked the seven-year anniversary of my dad's death. My dad was diagnosed with cancer in April and died in August. Relay is a way for me to give back to my dad by helping to raise money for cancer research.

On August 9, after Relay cleanup, I went home to bed. My husband had other plans. Our church was getting a new pastor, and today was move-in day. So instead of sleeping, Donnie went to help with the moving and then spent the afternoon doing some wiring and maintenance in the pastor's new home. Checking in on him once I was up, I could see he was in his goofy, lack-of-sleep mood. Pastor Doug must have been thinking, *What a goofball!* I tried my best to get him to come home for a nap; later that night, we had to help with a wedding at church.

With no nap before the wedding, Donnie had now been up forty-eight hours without sleep. After wedding cleanup, I wanted to go to the wedding dance for a while. I tried to convince Donnie to go, but he wouldn't. He was tired and irritable by this point, but that didn't seem to be the reason he wouldn't go. I told him I was going to go for a bit and not to worry, I was sure I could find someone to dance with me.

Normally, Donnie would have found this joke amusing. Not this time. He became angry, and when I left for the dance, we weren't speaking to each other. I didn't enjoy myself and left shortly after getting there. Donnie was not home when I got there. This confused me since he was so sleep deprived at the time.

The next morning, Donnie came into the bathroom where I was getting ready for church. He looked like he still had not slept. I noticed immediately that he was very emotional and seemed very upset. He started saying things about not being content, not doing what God wanted him to do. He asked me then, in tears, if I had been faithful in our marriage. I was appalled that he could ask me such a thing.

Being unfaithful had never crossed my mind. I don't know when he thought I would have the time to be unfaithful with three daughters, my first full-time teaching job approaching, and helping with the children's ministries at church. He knew where I was every second of every day. I was hurt that he had asked. I had loved Donnie since I was fifteen and been happily married to him for almost twenty-one years. Yet I could hardly be angry. Donnie was sobbing, telling me how disappointed he was with himself, our finances, and his life.

I was concerned. I felt his behavior was justifiable since he was on his third day of no sleep. I didn't know it then, but that is when my growing pains began. My comfortable world was about to turn upside down.

CHAPTER 2

Confusion

My husband's behavior sent me from concerned to confused. Things did not improve. I kept thinking as soon as he got some sleep, he would be fine. But he wasn't sleeping. I would wake up in the middle of the night and he would be gone. He wouldn't return until early morning. I would question him about his whereabouts. He would tell me that he wasn't tired, so he would get up and walk around town, stopping in front of people's houses, praying for them.

Donnie also wasn't eating. He wasn't hungry, ever. Sometimes, he would make himself eat. His food choices changed also. He went from liking spicy food to craving food so hot that he would be sweating bullets. One morning, I watched in silence as he put hot sauce on his cereal. Then he began an "all-natural kick." When he did eat, he ate a lot, and the only thing going in was all natural. He would not consider any medications, not even Tylenol for a headache. And he was adamant about our kids not taking any medications. He was constantly on all of us about eating "all-natural."

Other changes were taking place as well. My husband has never been much of a romantic, but all of a sudden, he was over the top with it. For my fortieth birthday, he showed up at my school with a bouquet of forty roses. He had picked up our youngest daughter Lexi, and the two of them were both dressed like clowns. I had rarely received flowers in our twenty-one years of marriage so this threw me. That wasn't all. A few days later, a new vehicle appeared in the driveway, used but new to us. Another birthday gift that I didn't feel we could afford.

All in all, I was being treated like a princess: gifts, massages, and praise. It would have been wonderful if I wasn't so confused by it. Everywhere we went, Donnie told everyone how wonderful I was. If this behavior and attention had always been, then it wouldn't have confused me so much. Donnie had always been a wonderful husband, but he had never been the romantic type. Every day, I became more convinced that something was terribly wrong.

CHAPTER 3

Mania

By September, I was terrified and drained. Donnie became very spastic. I became obsessed with researching the Internet. I was starting to lean toward bipolar. If I was right with my diagnosis, then Donnie was for sure in his manic stage. His energy level increased daily, and still, he wasn't sleeping. I became exhausted.

To have a conversation with him these days was like watching a two-hour movie in fast forward, with the volume as loud as it would go. In a one-minute conversation, Donnie would change topics a dozen times. He was all over the place. Sometimes, he would grab his head with his hands and say,

"Oh, the ideas are coming so fast, I can't think this fast." This became a common action of his.

I felt like every ounce of energy he gained was being sucked straight out of me. I had been in my teaching job for a few weeks now. Staying focused was work, and every ounce of energy I had left from dealing with the situation at home was put toward my new job. I quickly started to run on empty.

People around me started to notice changes. My mom immediately saw the change when she was visiting. I talked to her on the phone daily. She lives five hours away and she became my lifeline. She was doing her own research and was also leaning toward bipolar. On our daily visits, she would tell me how he needed help, a doctor, a psychologist. I got tired of hearing what I already knew and at times didn't even want to call. But I did, every day. I had never needed my mother more. I knew and believed what she was saying, but could not convince Donnie to get help.

Our close friends, Tommy and Beth, saw the changes. Tommy and Donnie were linemen together. Tommy had tried talking to Donnie, but he wouldn't listen. Tommy talked to me, telling me what he was seeing at work. It was what I myself was seeing at home. Tommy told me that Donnie was disappearing for long periods of time at work, long stretches where he was missing and no one knew where he was. He was close to being in trouble with his boss. It was time for me to confront him.

One day, I brought him to the computer. I pulled up the symptoms of bipolar. He read through the information, and several times, he would say, "I have that symptom and that one." He agreed to having over half the symptoms listed.

I asked him if we could get help. He told me he didn't need help, that all of this was coming from God. He said he had never felt better. When he disappeared at work, he was visiting people, people with depression, people who were sick, people who were down on their luck. Tommy and I both explained to him that he could not be doing that during work hours. He agreed to stop, but again said everything was coming from God. Every day, he was reading his Bible. Every day, he became more and more "religious."

New sayings started coming out. Every time I became upset, he looked at me with his now wild eyes and would say, "Egbok!" which was his new word for everything's gonna be okay. He talked a lot about how "people were wired." He would tell me it was okay if I wasn't on board with the new Donnie. It wasn't "how I was wired."

Suddenly, all of Donnie's energy was on people, especially hurting people. Donnie had always been a people person and would do anything to help anyone. But this was over the top. He was out to save the world, or at least the town we lived in. The ideas came fast. Donnie suddenly thought it was his job, that God was telling him, to confront everybody. He was getting involved in issues that did not involve us in any way. He was sticking his nose into everybody's business and offending many people.

Our church family was noticing the changes. Most people reacted by going the other direction when they saw us coming. This hurt, and I started to feel very alone.

I went out very little. Running to the store became a huge inconvenience. I love people and have always been very social. Now, I just wanted to hide. Everywhere I went, people would question me. The more I became introverted, the more Donnie made his presence known. He was talking and saying crazy things. Each time I went out, I was bombarded with off-the-wall questions. The things people were saying to me had to have come from my husband because too much information matched up.

For example, "So sorry to hear you're moving." When I said we weren't moving, I heard, "Oh, Donnie said he was moving to Arizona to work with his uncle." I knew he had to have told them this because this person had no way of knowing that Donnie really had an uncle in Arizona.

Other things I heard were that we were selling our house and buying a big old farmhouse and adopting a lot of children. I heard that we were opening a restaurant. The list went on and on. Donnie also started to mention his desire to cage fight. This terrified me, and thank goodness, he never followed through with it.

Another thing that was scaring me to death was his desire to help people. I have always been one to lend a hand,

and I knew God had slowly been working on my heart toward helping hurting people. But when I heard Donnie tell someone that he wasn't really interested in making any money himself but just in helping people, I got scared. With his new revelation came many ideas into a head that was already on overload.

Donnie was going to buy an old gas station and convert it into a restaurant because he knew of three or four ladies who wished they could open an eating establishment. He looked at an old school and started planning to turn that into a boys' home for troubled youth. He started visiting dairies because he wanted to start one and give every unemployed Hispanic person he knew a job. His helpfulness became very extreme. He came across one guy who needed to get rid of his dog. Donnie felt it his obligation to "help" this person. In no time at all, the dog came to live with us, destroying everything in its path. Donnie justified this by giving the dog to our daughter Taylor as a birthday gift. He said she had asked for a dog; she had not.

Then there were the inventions. Ideas were coming so fast into his head. His thoughts seemed to be clear, precise, and detailed. After he had several ideas, he actually contacted some patent companies, and phone calls and information started pouring in. He was missing for hours. During these times, he was out trying to find people to "fund" his ideas.

Other weird things were happening too. One day, Donnie was picking up some groceries, and he found a clearance shelf. He came home with eleven boxes of lemon instant pudding. No one at our house likes lemon pudding, but it was on sale and the store needed to get rid of it. He wanted to help them out.

Donnie's energy level increased daily while mine dwindled down to nothing. I felt I could barely put one foot in front of the other. Every day, I dreaded getting up, dreaded coming home from work, and dreaded my very existence. My life was spinning out of control.

CHAPTER 4

Juan

On September 11, 2009, I checked my phone during my break at work. I was frantic when I heard Donnie on my voice mail, sobbing, barely able to talk. He said he was just checking on me. He was alone on a gravel road at work. He said, all of a sudden, a crushing feeling in his chest had come over him. He said something bad was going to happen. He told me to check on the girls and to be careful driving home. I found out later that he had also called his foreman at work and told him of his concerns.

What do you do with a message like that? My concentration was gone for the day. Even though I was starting to see my husband as crazy more and more each day, I did call and check on my girls. By the end of the day, I had decided that Donnie was somehow relating the September 11, 2001, terrorist attacks with that day which was also September 11. That had to be it.

That night, we were at home when our oldest daughter Taylor called from a football game and said that Juan had been killed in a car accident. Donnie had coached Juan in high school wrestling, had coached his brother Jose, and was now coaching his brother, Julio. Donnie was devastated. The next day, we would find out that Juan's car accident had happened two miles down the road from where Donnie had felt that horrible crushing feeling in his chest, where he had felt that something bad was about to happen. The accident happened about four hours after he had left the message on my voice mail. Could God be talking to Donnie?

The next day, we went to Juan's sister's house to visit the family. We met Juan's mother. Donnie went to her and hugged her, both of them crying. He introduced himself as one of Juan's wrestling coaches. Months later, Juan's mother would tell me a story of a dream. She had this dream every night for two weeks before Juan's death. In her dream, she would be crying but not know why. At the end of each dream, a crying man would walk up to her and hug her. Then she would wake up. She told me that day when Donnie got out of the car and walked to her crying, it was just like her dream. Though they hadn't met until that moment, Donnie's face was the face of the man in her dream.

Juan's death was heartbreaking. Donnie played a huge part in putting together a funeral at our church with Pastor Doug. The forty roses I had gotten a few days earlier for my birthday made a beautiful casket spray. The funeral was beautiful, but one of the saddest I have ever been to.

Through all the planning for the funeral, all the sadness, I couldn't stop thinking about the frantic phone call from Donnie. I couldn't stop thinking about where Juan's accident took place, just down the road from where Donnie made that call. I couldn't stop thinking of Juan's mother's dream, the one that Donnie was in before she had ever laid eyes on him. I started to doubt my sanity. Maybe I was crazy and everything Donnie said was true, maybe God was telling him all of this. And if that was the case, then I was ignoring God.

CHAPTER 5

New Faces

By October, Donnie had introduced several new people into our home. Brian who, at the time I met him, was homeless; Julio, Juan's brother; and Sean, who I already knew, all started hanging out more at our house.

Yes, Donnie was into people, helping everyone. In the meantime, his manic behavior was pushing his family away. I wasn't thrilled having extra people around all the time when I was so stressed out about my life being such a mess. It was extra work for me as a few of the guys showed up regularly at mealtime and stayed into evening when my girls were trying to do homework and get ready for bed.

Donnie was starting to mention moving people into our basement. He talked about homeless people, about several Spanish people who were floundering around from place to place. This terrified me. All three of our daughters' bedrooms were in the basement. He was mentioning it daily, and I knew it was only a matter of time before he moved someone in there. When I would talk to him and disagree with him, he would become agitated. Then Donnie and I met Josh. Josh was a young single Christian man who had just moved to our town for his first teaching job. Josh and Donnie started doing a Bible study together in our garage.

Donnie became very adamant about moving someone into our house. We were full with no extra bedrooms, but when he suggested Josh, I agreed. I had met Josh and he was one of those people whom I immediately knew I could trust living in the basement with my daughters. At the time, I was only trying to pacify my husband. Later, I would come to depend on Josh very much. He quickly became a big brother to my daughters, and at times, he would become my life saver.

Donnie's manic behavior increased. He was convinced that everything was coming from God. I had to admit some really great things were happening. Sean had accepted Christ at a youth outing Donnie had asked him to help with. One night, a young man he had met came to our house and announced that he was at rock bottom. He had a noose in his car and planned to use it later that night. Donnie was able to talk him through that situation, and soon, that young man started attending church.

Donnie also began spending a lot of time with Julio. I didn't know Julio well, I had only been around him a few times, and I thought he was a really sweet kid, quiet, and very polite.

At the time Julio's brother Juan was killed in the accident, Julio had been living with him. Juan had been Julio's guardian as their mom lived in Chicago. After Juan's death, Julio moved in with his sister. He also became very dedicated to wrestling, and since Donnie was one of his coaches, they spent a lot of time together. Donnie started taking Julio to youth group and Julio also accepted Christ through Donnie's willingness to spend time with him.

Donnie started picking up hitchhikers whenever he saw one. In particular, one of the gentlemen he picked up needed a car. Donnie and Pastor Doug had set this gentleman up at the church for the night. Donnie came home and informed me that he was going to give this gentleman one of our cars. I was hysterical and instantly on the bed, unable to breath. You can't just give away a car to a stranger. Of course, this brought me countless lectures on not helping others, not behaving in a Christian manner, and, of course, how much more in tune Donnie was with God than I was. I gave up. Give the car away and keep paying the insurance. In the end, the man was able to fix his car enough to get to where he was going. He didn't need our car after all; I was relieved.

So yes, some good things were happening. Who was I to say that all that was going on with my husband wasn't coming from God? I had been saved when I was twenty-three but had not grown in my faith at all. I didn't feel that I really had a personal relationship with God, and Donnie declared that he was communicating directly with Him. He was even talking about going to seminary. And Donnie was not afraid to point out that he was closer to God than I was. He continually harassed me about my spiritual life and how mine wasn't measuring up compared to his.

In my heart, I knew that even though some good things had happened, not all of it was from God. Donnie started to become very hard on our oldest daughter Taylor; at times, he would be very mean to her. Kaylee, our middle daughter, was all of a sudden being doted on by her father. She quickly started to side with him on everything.

And then, I knew for sure. The mania was still there, but something else started to overcome it—anger.

CHAPTER 6

Moo

By the end of October, I was experiencing full-blown panic attacks. These usually left me in a heap on the floor, unable to breath. I remember Donnie and I having an argument once, I ended up on the floor, struggling for breath. Donnie looked down at me and told me if I wanted the panic attacks to stop, I needed to get right with God. Then he walked away. The panic attacks were very scary and also painful. Once I went to the ER, thinking I was having a heart attack. After that, I made myself an appointment and got some pills for anxiety. This helped take the edge off.

Also by October, Donnie was starting to talk about quitting his job. He just didn't think he wanted to be a lineman anymore. He was the next person in line for foreman, and that promotion was coming up. He was adamant about all the job offers that he had coming in from other sources. He had shared about a dozen of these with me, and I knew that if he gave up his lineman job and took one of these other jobs, we would never make it financially.

He started to talk a lot about raising Holstein calves. He talked about the Holstein operation that my dad used to have. He said God was telling him to raise these calves and to raise them using all-natural products. He wanted me in on this project. I didn't understand how I could. I was up at five every day just to get to work on time. Working out of town, I wasn't home until around 4:30. When was I going to find time to raise calves?

Donnie started researching it, located a place to start up, and just kept pushing. The more I said no, the more agitated he was becoming. For the first time, I was starting to fear my husband. I could see the anger, ready to boil over.

Once when we were arguing about it, he told me either I went along with his ideas or he wanted a divorce. This threw me a curve. On one hand, I would be happy and relieved to get out of the situation I was in. On the other hand, I knew my Donnie was in there somewhere, I knew in my heart this wasn't really him. And how could I make it on my own as a single mom?

I decided to agree to the calves on a small scale. Donnie wanted to start with 100 bottle calves. I was able to talk him down to under a dozen. Josh was a farm kid and also was showing some interest in helping with the calves. I decided that if Donnie had the calves for a hobby, maybe he would stop the talk about quitting his job.

CHAPTER 7

Ultimatum

The calves were cute. And they did make me smile. Taylor, by this time, had a lot of anger toward her dad and she wanted nothing to do with the calves. Josh and I helped out with them. On a regular basis, Donnie brought kids, adults, people who were hurting out to see and help with the calves. He viewed this as a mission field.

By now, living in our house, Josh started to question Donnie's behavior, especially the way he was treating Taylor. I could see him watching, his face remaining expressionless. I felt it was time he and I had a talk. I needed Josh on my side. We talked at length and Josh agreed something wasn't right. I knew that he would be praying. Other than my mom and my best friend Lisa, Josh was the only other person I had confided in with all the details.

Soon after, our dear friends Tommy and Beth stopped in to visit. They walked in the door and ask if they could talk to Donnie and me in the basement. I sat in silence as they talked to him about what was going on. They had noticed all the things I had noticed. Donnie became defensive. He asked me in front of them if I agreed with all they had said. I sat in silence, afraid to say anything. This enraged Donnie and he stormed to the garage. After Tommy and Beth left, I fearfully went to talk to Donnie. He was slamming things around. That is when he gave me the ultimatum.

Donnie told me then that if I didn't go along with all of his ideas, then he wanted a separation. He told me that he would not choose me over God and told me again that God was giving him all of his ideas. Again, I was weighing my options. I could get out, walk away. But common sense told me I couldn't make it with three kids, working out of town. And since Donnie was so freely leaving work to pursue other interests, I feared that he would disappear with Lexi. She was four at this time. I was stuck.

After the incident, his anger exploded and became part of our lives. Destroying the garage, throwing things, and smashing things, became a regular event. Within a few weeks' time, you could not walk through our garage, let alone get a vehicle in there. The gentle teddy bear man I married was gone. The girls and I walked around on eggshells whenever he was home. Thank goodness, that wasn't often.

By November, Donnie was more than in trouble at work. He continued to disappear for long periods of time. He developed paranoia about his coworkers and safety issues. He would come home frantic about safety issues he had seen. I talked to Tommy. He said there were no safety issues. He said the things Donnie was explaining were exaggerated and distorted.

Right about that time, Donnie's cousin became very ill. She had been fighting cancer for several years. We stopped in at the hospital to visit on a weekend when we were in our hometown. While at the hospital, Donnie decided he was going to stay. He had me call his boss to tell him. His boss questioned me since it was a cousin and not a direct relative. I also was confused. Donnie had been close to his cousin growing up, but not much since they were adults.

I was relieved. Relieved to drive away and leave him behind, relieved to have a few days of peace. I had hopes that his family would see his behavior and contact me to offer help. Yes, I would have the worry of caring for the baby calves, but I needed a break from what was now my life. I was tired, very tired.

Donnie was gone for a week or so. His cousin passed away shortly after he had returned home. Since I had left him in our hometown with no transportation, his mom's husband had let him borrow his motorcycle for the five-hour drive back. Once Donnie heard of his cousin's passing, he decided to head back to our hometown. I tried to get him to wait and go the day before the funeral. This was making no sense to me. If he waited, then I could attend the funeral, but having a brand-new job, I couldn't be gone most of a week. He wouldn't consider it. He was packing to leave when I left for work one morning. He was angry that I wouldn't take the time off to go with him. That day marks the greatest fear that I had during this whole ordeal: a terror that I will never forget.

CHAPTER 8

Terror

I had only been on the road headed to work for five minutes when Donnie called me. He had decided he was taking Lexi with him for the funeral. I was very uncomfortable with this. Donnie had always been one of the greatest dads I knew, but now, I felt his reasoning had left him. He had become reckless.

When he made the announcement, panic seized me. I played it cool and asked him if he had found other transportation. He was instantly irritated and reminded me he was taking the motorcycle. I told him he couldn't take Lexi on the motorcycle, she was only four, and it was a five-hour drive. His agitation grew and his reply was, "She'll have on a helmet."

To this day, I can tell you exactly where I was on my ride to work. Not a time goes by that I drive past that spot without being reminded. I slammed on the breaks. My hands were shaking, I couldn't breathe. I begged him to reconsider, to leave Lexi home. He wouldn't hear of it. The only helmet we had was a bicycle helmet. If Donnie had been in his right frame of mind, he would maybe have taken Lexi down the street for a short ride. He would have done this with much caution and little speed. Traveling on highways and interstates would have been out of the question, especially without a helmet.

I'm not sure how long I sat there, trying to weigh my options. Going home to try to stop him was sure to agitate him. I quickly called Taylor. She hurriedly told me that she knew of her dad's plans. She was doing her best to convince Lexi that she wanted to go to the babysitter's house. A bit later, Taylor confirmed that her dad had left on the motorcycle by himself. Taylor had gotten Lexi out the door to the sitters, and Donnie had lost focus and left without her.

What made Donnie change his mind that day? Did he lose focus; did he think it through? I think God clearly intervened. I was starting to realize that this wasn't the first time, nor would it be the last. I realized then that God was with me during this trying time and He would not leave me. I began to pray like I had never prayed before. Very quickly, I realized that I could feel God's presence with me. When I would cry out for desperate help, I would feel God's peace come over me. This would be a physical feeling that started at the top of my spine and worked its way down, almost like a shiver. It didn't happen once or twice, it happened every time I begged God to help me. I was not alone.

Daily, I talked to my mom, and daily, I talked through e-mail with my best friend Lisa. I was able to confide in Josh and often visited with Tommy and Beth. I couldn't have made it through without those people, but all they could do is listen. Soon I would ask others for help, family members that I thought might be able to get through to Donnie, convince him he needed help. But those pleas were ignored. Yes, my new relationship with God would have to keep me strong. It was all I had.

CHAPTER 9

Betrayal

By mid-November, Donnie's anger was becoming more violent, more explosive. I was scared of him, scared he would hit me. Even though I was scared, part of me wanted him to hit me. I felt it was my only way out. I felt I couldn't do it anymore. I was desperate for help. My mom, Lisa, Josh, and Tommy and Beth had all tried to help. Dawn, a secretary at Donnie's work, stopped by often, in tears, and tried to convince Donnie to get help. I had also confided in my boss at work. Soon after that, my students started asking me questions about things they never could have known unless the information had leaked. This was very frustrating for me as I worked in a Christian school.

I still had the panic attacks, even though I was praying daily. I knew, despite them, that God was with me. I finally stopped questioning why this was happening to our family.

Before Donnie's cousin passed away, I was desperate enough to finally ask for help from some of Donnie's family members. Several times, I started to dial the number, several times, I hung up. Then Donnie's cousin died and I didn't feel the time was right. My mom must have felt my desperation. She took it upon herself to show up at Donnie's dad's work. She told him exactly what was going on.

Later, Mom called me to tell me what she had done. She apologized, but I felt no anger. What I did feel was relief. Finally, I was going to get some help from someone that I thought Donnie might listen to.

My relief was short lived. Donnie's dad called me and I remember being told that I was imagining or exaggerating. After all, while Donnie was in our hometown during his cousin's illness, they had been around him a lot. They said they had seen none of the symptoms I had described. His dad admitted Donnie had talked about a job change, and though he didn't understand it and hated to see it, if Donnie wanted a change, there was nothing anyone could do. From the conversation I gathered, they thought we were having marital problems and that I was trying to get them on my side. His dad made it clear that they did not want to get involved.

They had been my last hope. The person I thought could convince Donnie to not leave his job and get some help didn't believe me. Were they blind? How could anyone spend time around Donnie and not see the drastic manic behavior?

I remember the sinking feeling of helplessness. I had gone to our pastor several times. The problem was the day he moved to town was the day my world turned upside down. He had only briefly met Donnie before that day. He had nothing to go on. He thought Donnie's behavior was normal for him.

I was relieved to have Donnie out of town, though I wished the reason was other than a funeral of a very young woman. I knew his return was just around the corner. I felt betrayed by Donnie's family members. At this point, I had only contacted his dad. I didn't talk to his mom because I wasn't sure she would believe me. She holds her son on a pretty high pedestal. Besides, I knew that if she did believe me, she would be calling every day in tears and I couldn't handle that.

A few days later, Donnie's dad called me. "Okay, I've seen the behavior you described, what can I do to help?" The relief was, again, short-lived. I didn't hear from him much after his offer to help. I found out later that they had decided to stick with their decision of not getting involved. I was alone. I had already researched how to have someone committed. There was no way to do it unless he had a gun to his head or was suicidal. Or if he committed himself, but I knew that would never happen. I checked into getting a restraining order. Again, there was no help. Until he hit me or the girls, it was useless.

CHAPTER 10

The Counselor

Donnie quit his job, gave his notice. He would be done in a few weeks. His work encouraged him to see a counselor. They all knew this behavior was not normal, but no one was getting through to him. He agreed to the counselor, and they set him up with a Christian organization. I appreciated this last ditch effort and had another glimmer of hope.

The evening we went, I realized Donnie was excited about this counseling session. He couldn't wait. The counselor was a very nice man, obviously a Christian. He would surely see Donnie's manic behavior and suggest some help.

We went in together and Donnie was given the floor. He told the counselor how all these great ideas were coming to him and how they were coming from God. He was in his manic mode, full force, barely coming up for air. Finally, someone was going to tell Donnie what I already knew, he needed help.

Next, it was my turn. I told him everything from the beginning, every tiny detail. By the time I was finished, I was fighting a panic attack. We were wrapping up, and I anxiously awaited the diagnosis. Was it bipolar, was it a chemical imbalance? Would he suggest committing him?

I still get tears in my eyes remembering what came next. The counselor looked at Donnie and told him he was jealous. He said he had longed to directly communicate with God and see such direct leading like Donnie obviously was getting.

Shooting pain began in my head, like a knife going in and out. My vision became fuzzy. That very second, I was thrown into a migraine. The only thing I really remember about the rest of the meeting was the counselor talking to Donnie like I wasn't there about how he could fill all of his desires of different job opportunities and helping people. I remember the counselor telling him to do these things but slow down a bit and give his wife time to accept them.

From what I was hearing in the rest of the conversation, I had become the crazy one. And I started to think that maybe, just maybe, they were right. On top of the anxiety and panic attacks, I began getting sores on my head. I knew they were caused from stress as that is when they popped out. They were itchy and painful. I knew I couldn't take much more.

CHAPTER 11

Thanksgiving

For Thanksgiving, we headed to family in our hometown as usual. By this time, Donnie was at the top of his manic phase. His job was done, and he was ready for new adventures. I was not excited about going home. A five-hour drive stuck in a car with a crazy man, fearing for all our lives because of how he had begun to drive fast and recklessly. Then spending time acting like everything was fine. I wasn't excited at all.

The trip home was a disaster as far as family seeing what my life had become. On my side, everyone noticed the manic behavior. I received all kinds of advice on what I needed to do. I know everyone meant well, but I didn't need anyone telling me Donnie needed medical treatment. I fully knew that and couldn't do anything about it.

The weekend was stressful to say the least. My family hounding me about getting Donnie help and being offended by every off-the-wall thing he said and did. Donnie's family said nothing. At times, I'd see a look of concern cross his mom's face, but she didn't question anything. I remember going to his dad's: nothing. Didn't they care? Fine if they didn't want to help me, but what about their grandchildren? What about their own son?

Other than the stress, a few things stood out about the weekend. Donnie went hunting and shot his first deer. This stands out to me because for the next several months, that dead bloody deer would hang in our garage. The dog Donnie had brought home ripped it apart, scattering pieces everywhere. Donnie cut meat off it to cook for himself, and eventually, the carcass smelled up the whole garage.

The other thing was Donnie had been in touch with Julio who was going to be alone during most of the Thanksgiving weekend. Donnie wanted him to bring our extra car to our hometown and join us. I agreed so as not to anger Donnie. I admit I did feel a little tug on my heart. I was sad that Julio would be alone for the holiday.

This was a very big step in my growing pains. That weekend, I grew very fond of Julio. I was feeling something, something I couldn't describe. Different than the anger and fear that I had felt almost nonstop since August, this was something that later I would realize was God Himself tugging on my heart.

CHAPTER 12

A Change

Without a job, Donnie had time to pursue inventing. He contacted patent companies again to discuss his many ideas. He spent his days out and about, talking to people about all the promised job opportunities. As I had feared, no job opportunities were available. Donnie didn't seem concerned. We cashed in half of his retirement to live on. I wasn't happy about this, but it was our only option with him not working.

The trials and fear of this time brought about some changes. The manic phase was slowing down. The anger was still there, but not as violent. Something was changing, but I wasn't sure what it was. Looking back, I think Donnie realized what he had done, quitting his job. I think he realized the other "job opportunities" had fallen through.

I became very resentful. I started watching the papers, ready to take on a night job. The retirement money would run out soon with Donnie not working. It was only a matter of time before we lost everything we had.

CHAPTER 13

Bad News

December 30, Donnie walked through the door after wrestling practice. His face was grey and he was close to tears. He told me that Julio hadn't shown up at practice. Donnie had tried to call, thinking he had overslept. No answer. Donnie went to Julio's sister's house. There was no one there. Donnie knew something was wrong. One of Julio's friends came to Donnie and told him that Julio had been arrested the night before for shoplifting.

When Donnie told me this, I felt that tugging on my heart again. In those few seconds while I processed the news, I had a realm of emotions run through my veins. I wanted nothing to do with a Hispanic kid who had shoplifted. Nonetheless, the tug became stronger, and I instantly knew that I was supposed to leave with Donnie right then and head to the town where Julio was being held.

Visiting someone in jail was new to us, and we arrived to find we could see him during visiting hours only. We were told he was on immigration hold. We didn't understand exactly what that meant but thought maybe it was because Julio's resident card had been lost during Juan's accident.

For the first time in months, I looked into Donnie's eyes and saw him in there. It was his eyes, not the wild and sometimes angry eyes. At that moment, it's like nothing had gone wrong over the last few months. We agreed then and there to do whatever it took to help Julio out of this mess.

The next day, we finally got to visit Julio, through the glass and over a phone. I remember that moment so clearly. Julio looked so young and scared; he looked so ashamed. I tried to fight that physical feeling tugging on my heart. That very moment, I fell head over heels in love with a kid I hardly knew.

We visited every day that there were visiting hours and twice on Sundays. We were on the phone nonstop with the parole officer and immigration services. Slowly, things started to come together. This was not Julio's first offense but his second. The first time he was picked up was before Juan's death. We were willing to post bail, but Julio was on ICE hold. Immigration had a hold of him and there was little we could do. After two weeks, Julio was moved to another town, farther from us, and we were only able to visit him every other week or so. There was a great possibility that Julio would be deported. Julio was a legal resident, but not a citizen. We were told that the law was harder on the residents than on citizens or even illegals.

By this time, Donnie and I had become totally consumed with helping Julio. I had been on Christmas break from school and would soon return. We had talked to an attorney. She was an immigration attorney and not cheap by any means.

The phone calls from Julio became fewer and fewer. When he did call, he was really down. Julio's main concern was missing his wrestling season. That was one of the few things in life that mattered to him.

Finally, court day was here. We went into a small immigration office, which was crowded. Everybody in there was sad and scared. We were told that there was no way to predict the outcome of what would happen that day. The judge was known as hardcore. We had agreed to have Julio live with us when he was released, and the attorney thought this would work in his favor. The attorney soon got us in for a visit with Julio. We hadn't seen him for a few weeks.

During the time that we waited for our turn in court, they seemed to forget that we were visiting with Julio. Our ten minutes turned into an hour. During this time, Julio seemed to be at rock bottom and he began to open up about his childhood. He remembered some of his younger years living in Mexico and crossing into the United States. Life didn't get a lot easier once he was here. All of the information I have gotten over the years of getting to know Julio is enough to fill a book all on its own. But that is not my book to write. Someday, I hope Julio or his mom will write down all the details of their hardships and share them with the world. For me, the sad, sad story of Julio just strengthened my love for him, made me want to protect him with everything in me.

Finally, our turn in the courtroom came. We were ushered in. I was shaking so badly and already crying. Julio came in, orange jumpsuit and shackled. The prosecutor was fighting hard to have Julio deported. The judge was not kind, but he seemed fair. We won. Julio was released. Bond was very high, and he would have to report to his parole officer and do community service.

Donnie and I waited a couple hours for the completion of all the paperwork for Julio's release. During this time, I felt such joy. I remember Donnie looking at me and saying, "Don't celebrate here. Look around, we are the only ones getting good news." That is when I started to pay attention to what was going on around me. The room was tiny, not enough chairs to seat everyone. A pop machine took up a large portion of the room. We heard someone comment that the pop machine was the only one for the whole floor of the building. Constantly employees were coming in and out for pop. The pop machine was loud, and the employees were louder.

Everyone waiting was crying. From watching, I soon figured out what most people were doing there. They were bringing their loved ones their belongings for when they were deported. Each person being deported was allowed a very small bag, which could include no money and no electronics. Over and over, I watched people bring in the bag they had packed so carefully and see it dumped and gone through by the immigration workers. Then things were shoved back into the bag and what they couldn't get in this time went to the trash. There was no respect in this process.

Something else I noticed was that in the immigration office, all employees spoke English. No one, not one person, spoke Spanish or any other language. The people being deported and the family members bringing the belongings didn't understand anything being said. Our attorney, as well as several other attorneys, spent any free time they had trying to interpret for people who were not even their clients. The whole immigration process was very inhumane.

We were the first ones there that morning and the last ones to leave when the office closed. I was convinced we were the only ones to get good news that day. Like I said before, I could write a whole book on Julio alone, but that is not what I'm here to tell you about now. We got Julio home; he moved in with us. Our next confrontation came with the school board. They voted that Julio was not allowed to finish his senior year of wrestling. He was devastated.

When we asked Julio to live with us, Donnie was still on the downside of a manic phase. Donnie promised Julio to love him like a dad, a dad that he never had. Unfortunately,

Donnie hit depression and that promise was broken. Julio lived with us for the next several years, and I might as well have been a single mom to him. I always knew that Donnie's broken promise had hurt and disappointed Julio deeply. I also knew that Julio blamed himself for Donnie's depression.

CHAPTER 14

More Changes

Many changes happened as Julio became a part of our family. I know that it was easier for our family to adjust than it was for Julio. Donnie's manic behavior was gone. His rage and angry outbursts were gone. He had seemed so focused, so normal during the time we were helping Julio. I felt a little hope that he was coming back to us.

Soon, Donnie began to regret quitting his job. He was feeling useless. All the job offers that he was sure he heard were not there. By then, we had sold our calves. Donnie's desire to raise the calves left with his mania. Very little money was coming in. I remember Donnie telling me back in his manic phase that he didn't need any certain kind of job. He would be content doing anything. It was very frustrating to me that he wasn't applying at the local grocery and convenience stores.

At this point, I was worrying about losing our house. I had called the mortgage company and explained the situation and asked if we could miss one payment. They told me that we had always paid on time and, of course, we could miss a payment as long as we made a double payment first. That isn't skipping a payment. I began searching frantically for a second job. I also began pushing Donnie in a very impatient and not so-nice way to get a job—any job.

For a while, Donnie was hired to work for a farmer with a baby Holstein operation. Although not a lot of money, a little was better than nothing. Every day that went by, I noticed a change in Donnie, a change that was not good.

CHAPTER 15

The Crash

He was slipping—fast. Before I knew it, Donnie had fallen into depression. It started with a lot of worrying about a job. Next came frequent tears and apologies for what he had done. He was realizing he had gotten us into what seemed like a hopeless mess.

In a matter of two weeks, Donnie was in a deep depression and had to quit his job with the farmer. I had heard about depression but never could I have imagined how awful it could be. One day, I came home to find Donnie had been in bed all day, blinds closed. That is the way our room stayed for the next month. Donnie stopped eating and he never came out of the bedroom. He cried all the time. He told me that he felt like he was in a deep, deep hole with no way out.

My anger quickly dissolved. I was scared. I felt like I did when I watched my dad die bit by bit every day. I was helpless to help my husband. I talked with Pastor Doug often. He advised me to remove all guns from our house. Donnie refused all phone calls. His mom, by now, knew what was going on. She called often in tears. I had no good news for her.

Pastor Doug came in almost daily to check on Donnie so I could keep working. He was the only person Donnie would see and that was because Doug just walked through the front door and into the closed bedroom.

After two or three weeks, Donnie started to look like he had just gotten out of a concentration camp. At times, I practically had to carry him to the bathroom. He was very weak. He told me that he lay there all day and prayed for death. He prayed that he had a tumor that had caused him to make all the poor decisions he had made over the last several months. He prayed that the tumor would take him.

Our girls must have been terrified. I thank God that Lexi was little and asked no questions when I told her Daddy was sick. Taylor had a few breakdowns at school and confided in some of her teachers. Kaylee was keeping all of her feelings bottled up. I continued to talk to my mom, and she continued to tell me I needed to get Donnie help. I helped Julio where I could, but he rarely came out of his room.

Before depression was at its worst, I had talked to Pastor Doug about having Donnie committed. He explained to me that the process would involve bringing Donnie into a room full of people he loved, leading him to a breaking point and getting him to agree to commit himself. I knew I couldn't do it.

One day, one of Donnie's sisters called and said Donnie needed to be committed, and that if I couldn't do it, she was willing to drive up and do it. This was frustrating for me. After months of begging that side of the family for help, now they offer? And they couldn't just come and commit him. He had to do it himself. I felt like I was being accused of not taking care of Donnie. They had no idea the hell we had been through. Deep inside, I knew she was only trying to help.

A few days after this, on a sunny Saturday afternoon, Donnie called me into the bedroom. He asked me if I would drive him to the hospital to be committed. He was ready for help. I called a hotline number in the phone book. I told them about the months of mania and now the depression. I told them that Donnie said he needed to be committed today, that he couldn't take it anymore, and that he needed help. The reply I got was, "I'm sorry, it is Saturday and we don't take new patients on Saturday." I had implied to the lady that he was suicidal and was asking for help. I had told her that I had tried and tried for months to get him help and was told that I couldn't until he committed himself. She suggested I call back Monday. By Monday, Donnie was no longer willing to commit himself.

CHAPTER 16

Breaking Point

Donnie reached his breaking point again all on his own. One day while I was working, he called Pastor Doug to say he couldn't take it anymore. He wanted Doug to take him to get help.

They went to the doctor that day. Donnie was declared clinically depressed and malnourished. He had lost twenty pounds in two weeks' time, and this was on top of all the weight he had lost when he was manic. Pastor assured me that in a few weeks, the antidepressant would kick in and my Donnie would return to me.

Slowly after a long two weeks, Donnie came back to life. He started to eat, then, the blinds opened in the bedroom for the first time in a month. Eventually, he came to the living room for short visits. He was very weak, but I could tell that he was going to be okay.

During this time of recovery, he got an unexpected visit from his dad and stepmom. They didn't call, they just showed up. I remember making my daily call at break to make sure Donnie was okay when he told me he had visitors. He asked me if I had asked his dad to come. He thought they had come to commit him. I assured him I was just as surprised as he was and that I knew nothing about it. After a short visit, they left. I was still very hurt and angry about their lack of interest in our lives over the past few months. I managed to stay away from the house until they were gone.

CHAPTER 17

Back to Normal
What Is Normal?

Our lives slowly evolved back to normal. Well, normal is not quite where we were. Donnie's heart seemed to have hardened with everything that had happened.

Once Donnie was feeling stronger, he tried holding down a few jobs. Those didn't work out. One involved middle of the night hours, and the other involved too much new information for him to process at that time. He finally got a construction job and worked there through the following fall.

One day, I called the Lineman Union Hall. I had called to ask them if there was any way he could get his lineman job back. I explained what had happened. I said I had wished they would have put him on a medical leave but understood why they had not. I was told that his company could not be forced to give his job back to him; however, the man on the phone told me that he could get Donnie line work, but he would have to travel.

When I explained to Donnie all of the information I had gotten, I saw mixed emotions on his face. He was not excited about working away from home, but I saw a glimmer of self-worth, something I hadn't seen in a while. Donnie was a good lineman, and the pay they were offering him was almost double what he had made before. He couldn't turn it down. We were close to financial ruin. Although not what either of us wanted, we really had no choice.

Donnie became my traveling lineman. This job seemed to bring new life into him. He began to feel pride in his job again, and it wasn't long before he was promoted to foreman.

CHAPTER 18

Growing Pains Are
a Good Thing!

Start to finish, Donnie was sick from August 2009 through August 2010. Then from September through November 2010, he was still gaining strength and trying to put his life back together.

Once he was better, he was willing to visit a doctor. The only thing that they could come up with left us with unanswered questions. The doctor said best he could figure out, Donnie skipping three nights sleep had thrown him into something. Something. That was our answer to so many questions.

Donnie doesn't remember a lot of things that he said and did during that time. When I told him about Lexi and the motorcycle incident, he cried. Going out in public was hard after he was better. This made going on the road a little easier for him. He had offended many and I think most people thought he was off his rocker!

Sometimes, Donnie would feel hurt that someone avoided him. That is when I would gently tell him what he had said to that person. Donnie started to meet with people he had wronged to apologize, to explain. Now, three years later, he still doesn't enjoy talking about it.

God used what we went through to grow me. I had no one that could help me, some tried but couldn't. I had no one but God alone. My growing season taught me about prayer, it taught me to fully rely on God, and it taught me to fully trust. He never left me. He never left Donnie. Through every terror, through every panic attack, He was right beside me.

God blessed us with daughters who have huge hearts. Donnie didn't remember how awful he had treated Taylor, and when I told him, he went to her in tears, asking forgiveness. Taylor hugged her dad and said, "I already forgave you a long time ago."

I feel like Julio was a huge part of my growing season. I believe God put him right in the middle of my living room to soften my hard judgmental heart. Loving Julio has taught me so much.

I feel we failed Julio. When Donnie was in his manic stage, he made a lot of promises to Julio. Depression came soon after those promises and they were never kept. Julio struggled with making good choices while he lived with us. I will always wonder if things would have been different if promises had been kept. On the flip side of that, if Donnie hadn't been manic, if I hadn't been at rock bottom, would we have decided to help a troubled boy we barely knew?

God is still growing me. My stubborn heart still holds a grudge and many hard feelings toward people who turned their backs when I was so desperate for help. I know I need to forgive and move on. God reminds me of this daily. God is patient. He knows I will have to endure more growing pains before I am ready for this step.

When Donnie was better, I told him that I stood by him once, but I would walk if it happened again. At the same time, I know God isn't finished with me yet. Growing pains aren't fun, but they are important. Donnie and I conquered the worst of the storms and I am here to stay.

CHAPTER 19

Today, I finish part 1 of my story. For a long time, I set the book aside, didn't touch it. It was too much to relive it as I typed. My growing season seemed to live on! While Donnie has been on the road, everything that could go wrong at our house has. We had to put in a new sewer system, we replaced countless appliances due to power surges from an ice storm, and we have had vehicle problems. Our oldest daughter Taylor had health issues that we could not pinpoint for many months. She ended up having to leave college. My being gone for her emergencies was frowned upon at my job, and I ended up leaving in the middle of the year on not very good terms.

Our middle daughter Kaylee has had countless health issues that continue today. I like to call her my walking medical nightmare. Julio completed high school and two years of college. We helped him through this time. He has continued to make poor choices and has caused much heartache. Yes, since Donnie was sick, it has been one thing after another—more growing pains for sure.

Donnie was healing from the season of manic and depression. I was healing. Our marriage seemed pretty much back to where it had been. We were slowly climbing out of the debt that we had. Donnie's illness brought about much financial difficulty. But he doesn't get all the blame for that. After his depression, he, for the first time, started to ask me about our finances. I had always paid all the bills. He had never asked any questions and I had never offered any information. I found it hard to tell him that when I went back to school to continue my education, I had to use credit cards to pay for part of my schooling. We also had credit cards that we had used together, and he had no idea on the amounts. I was wrong not to tell him all this information. Even if he hadn't asked, I should have offered it up. But I didn't. This came to be part of our growing pains. We worked hard at paying off all of our debt.

Donnie has continued to work on the road. He was fortunate enough to work near where his youngest brother Kadin and his family live, and they graciously let Donnie stay with them. They have a family and being around kids and family helped Donnie survive living on the road. For months, before moving in with them, he lived in hotels and that was a very lonely time for him.

Living with Kadin and Krista brought much healing for Donnie. He began to talk in length with them about his illness. In fact, they talked about it so much that they named his illness, George. Talking about George and other childhood hurts helped Donnie move forward. Having Krista to talk to also helped me heal.

Lexi has come to me lately with achy legs. I know from her high-water pants and huge appetite that she is experiencing growing pains. I can often lessen her pains with some Tylenol. Growing pains hurt, that is for sure, but they are necessary for growth.

Almost four years after Donnie's illness, after three years of working on the road, we saw him come back to us. For almost two weeks straight, I saw the man I married. His heart seemed right again, not hard. Two weeks. I noticed it, my girls noticed it. Finally, he was back. We had managed to pay off all of our credit cards, every last one, and we vowed never to touch them again. Things were going really well. Then one day, I sat down at my computer. I had a message from Krista. The message said, "We have noticed some manic behaviors in Donnie, and we were just wondering if you were seeing the same thing…"

PART 2

Growing Pains

CHAPTER 1

Denial

For two straight weeks, we had him back. For the past few years, we had gone through the motions. When Donnie was home on the weekends, we did nothing. We no longer had couple friends; that ended when Donnie went on the road. I felt that I had lost a lot of my friends when Donnie was manic. Life became very routine. Donnie worked during the week. I kept things up at home and made sure I had the laundry caught up by the weekend. Donnie would come home on Friday nights. I would do his laundry all weekend, and we would sit and do nothing. Life was boring, and when he was home, I seemed to be just as lonely as I was when he was gone. He seemed…blah. He existed, he worked, he visited on the weekends, he left, and it started over again. I can't say that I thought he was depressed over the last three years, just blah. There were no interests, no excitement, nothing. The only depression I knew about was what I saw him go through. I did not know enough about it to realize that over the last three years, the depression was still there.

Then, one weekend, he came home and I noticed a difference. I was watching a friend's little girl and Donnie actually paid attention to her, held her, played with her. She always tried to get Donnie's attention and could hardly get him to look her way. That weekend, he was more talkative, more involved. After he left Monday morning, the girls said they had noticed too. The following weekend, we noticed again. He was back.

That second Monday is when I got the message from Krista. She said that she and Kadin had seen some manic behavior in Donnie and wondered if I had noticed anything. I told her I hadn't; normally, by the time we saw him on the weekends, he was tired. I did mention that we had noticed a positive change, that we thought he was doing better.

That message came the week before Easter and I was on the lookout. For the last three years, on rare occasions when Donnie would get excited or be hyper, I would get a feeling of panic. Oh no, is it happening again? It didn't happen often, so I thought it was just Donnie being Donnie, the way he used to be. As I watched for anything that would remind me of four years ago, I was in denial. Anything I saw I believed was just Donnie coming back to us. But always, for a split second, I would be scared. Sometimes, Donnie would tell me that he felt like he was under a microscope. He felt like I and everybody else was always watching him, judging him.

We went home for Easter weekend, and right away, my mom questioned me. Again, I was in denial. When my mom asked, I told her that he was better, that this was the old Donnie.

A month later, we returned to our hometown for my niece's graduation reception. My denial came to a halt. Donnie was hyper; he was loud, obnoxious, and literally pinging off the walls. People were getting annoyed by his behavior. Please, God, not again.

On our way home, it began to storm. We had six people in our pickup and we came upon a bicyclist, an older gentleman, pedaling hard to get to the next town before the storms hit. We had taken this route to try to avoid the storms, but the sky was looking very scary. Donnie had started to pick up hitchhikers and I was totally against this, especially with my kids in the vehicle. Donnie suggested we stop to help this gentleman and I agreed. The storm looked like it would hit at any minute.

We offered help, he welcomed it, and we quickly loaded his bike in the back of our truck and squeezed him in. All the kids were in the back, Donnie was driving and our new passenger and I were up front with him. We quickly learned his story. He was from France, riding across the United States to raise money for his nephew who had a serious illness. He just needed to be taken to the next town. Donnie immediately decided he wanted to keep this adorable little man. He began telling the man that we would take him home with us, that we lived in a town that had lots of money, and he could resume riding from there.

Our passenger spoke English, but there was definitely a language barrier. He showed me his detailed itinerary and his schedule. He did not want this storm to alter any of that. We arrived at the town where he wanted to be dropped off and Donnie just kept driving. I leaned over and whispered that this was the town where he wanted out. Donnie said we couldn't just leave him on the street with a storm coming. I said, "Then leave him at a gas station, he wants out." The gentleman was very focused on his map and itinerary. He didn't realize we had gone right past his destination. I told Donnie to pull over. I asked the man to explain where he wanted out. I told him we had just gone through that town. He asked us to please turn around and take him back there. I looked at Donnie, beyond angry at this point. I remember my words, "You cannot kidnap this man, take him back to the town and let him out." The gentleman was adamant. Donnie finally gave in.

We left this sweet man at a rest area, cement floor, made of brick. He would be safe. Later, we would check his blog and see a picture we had taken with him. He would thank us and show everyone that we got him to safety. He had set up his tent right in the shelter and was snug as a bug.

This would go down as the first bizarre, I mean really bizarre, thing that this manic episode would bring about, a kidnapping of an old man. I remember telling our pastor about it and he laughed and laughed. Looking back now, it was funny. Donnie was only trying to help and just wanted to take the cute little man home with us and keep him forever. But in the big scheme of things, it wasn't funny. It was the beginning of what was coming.

CHAPTER 2

The Meeting

At the time I feared everything was starting back up again, Donnie was offered a job fifty minutes from home. This was an answer to prayer as he could be home each night. I remember texting my pastor to let him know and jokingly saying, "What if we can't live together after living apart for three years?" Well, I may have been joking, but living together full-time again was work, hard work.

Having Donnie home every night, I quickly noticed the manic behavior. It was not all the time. Four years ago, it started and got consistently worse daily. This time, it would come and it was pretty mild. Then it would disappear for days.

This caused me much doubt. I kept thinking I was imagining and I became very guilty of looking at my husband under that microscope he was so worried about.

I had been very open with Donnie about my fears. I asked Donnie if I could hold a meeting with a few of our closest friends to discuss my fears and what he had going on. He felt nothing was wrong and he quickly agreed. I set up the meeting at church. I invited our pastor and his wife, some dear friends Denny and Erma, and Donnie's close friend Paul. I had thought about inviting Tommy and Beth, but they had been so involved last time that I didn't want them there. I wanted everyone there to be neutral.

The meeting started with me telling everyone why I had asked them there. I told them that I was seeing some behaviors that reminded me of four years ago. Before I went any farther, I asked Donnie what he wanted to say. He talked about God directing him to get involved in people's lives. He explained how God had lately been bringing people into his path that he had been involved with four years ago. That is when I told Donnie to tell the group about the experience he had at Kadin and Krista's.

Donnie explained that he was lying in bed one night feeling really down. He was basically feeling like God had punished him for what happened four years ago. He said that God had directed him then, to reach out to certain people and Donnie started to do this but then forgot about God and went his own way. He explained that this led to his manic behavior and then he explained that God punished him with depression and then again by sending him on the road away from his family. He told the group that I had pulled him out of the depression, saved him from destruction. This was the first time that I had heard this explanation of what happened four years ago from him. He then went on to explain that he was getting a second chance from God to fix everything from four years ago. He also mentioned that four years ago, when our family was in great need, that our church looked the other way and did not get involved. This had hurt Donnie greatly.

He told them that one night as he lay in bed and cried out to God, he kept repeating, "Less of me and more of you, God." At that time, Donnie said he felt something in his feet. He described it like sparklers, bright, warm, and tingly. It started in his feet and slowly went up his body to the top of his head.

I wanted Donnie to share this because I fully believed it. And I wanted everyone to be neutral. I cannot explain how badly I wanted everyone in the room to say that this is for real, this is from God, calm down, Lori! I then took a turn to explain what I was seeing.

I explained in detail, the hyperness and the racing thoughts (though not as bad as before). I told the group that God really did seem to be bringing the same people across Donnie's path. I told them about the people who were led to Christ four years ago during Donnie's manic months. I explained how Donnie had been the last several years, no interest, no motivation, and all of a sudden, it had changed. I told them I had noticed that he was hoarding again, only worse than four years ago. Then, I got tears as I said, "Four years ago, it was hell, and I will not do it again."

Our group began to discuss things. A few things stick out to me. I clearly remember Donnie telling everyone how he had the best wife in the world for putting up with him four years ago and pulling him out of depression. This made me remember the praise and doting Donnie had showered on me during those months of mania. Normally, he wasn't so generous with his praise of me. I remember Lesleigh, Pastor Doug's wife, saying that she loved and admired Donnie's enthusiasm and love for people. She felt confident that God was getting ready to use Donnie in a big way. I remember Paul asking Donnie about the hoarding. He had noticed it as Donnie had a lot of "piles" at Paul's farm. Donnie, out of the blue, said that he was hoarding because God was telling him to prepare for end-times. This was the first I had heard this and asked him what he planned to do with all the throw-away power line poles he was hoarding. Were we going to eat those in end-times?

I remember Pastor Doug asking Donnie if he was a good leader in the household. This was said in innocence but would come back to haunt me for the next six months. The main thing I remember about that day is what Pastor Doug said at the end of the meeting. "I believe this could be God's leading.

But I also have to be able to look Lori in the eye three months from now and say we did all we could."

The meeting wrapped up with everyone promising to pray. Paul left with hugging us both and saying that it would all work out. God had a plan. Donnie left feeling confident. I left feeling very unsure of everything. I was still in the denial mode.

CHAPTER 3

New Job

Donnie began his new job and loved it. He talked about how serious they were about safety, how beautiful it was where he was working, and how great the guys were he worked with. He made comments like, "I feel guilty for getting paid. I love my job."

This went on for a few weeks. Then I started to hear about safety issues and not fitting in with the crew. I questioned him and reminded him that he had said his crew was great and that safety was a top priority. He just said that it was hard to be the new guy on a crew. He talked daily of the apprentices not respecting him. This struck me as odd right away. Donnie, being a journeyman lineman, had always, always treated the apprentices with respect and always felt it his duty to teach them, with kindness and patience, as they worked. I had heard countless stories on how others treated the apprentices badly and how they all loved working with Donnie because he was kind to them. Red flags were popping up in my mind. I was reminded of when he quit his lineman job four years ago. What he was telling me now was very similar to what he had said then.

Donnie became very irritable. He was easily set off. He left early each morning. I remember getting up with him in the early hours and making his lunch while he got his breakfast. Then I would go back to bed for an hour after he left. One morning, I had been back in bed for about ten minutes when I heard the door open. Donnie stormed into the bedroom and said he had forgotten his phone. His phone was attached to him like another arm these days. Contacts, he always had his phone because he was walking around getting "contacts," whatever that meant. He stormed into the room, grabbed his phone, and said to me, in a very mean voice, "I need more from you than a sandwich!" I didn't know what he meant by this, but it hurt my feelings. He apologized later, but his short fuse was another reminder of four years ago.

A few weeks later, Donnie was fired from his job. According to him, the apprentice had pushed his buttons and Donnie had retaliated. The apprentice turned him in and Donnie was fired the following day. Donnie felt this unjust and reported it to the union hall. This issue would drag on for months before Donnie let it drop. He managed to make many people angry over it.

Donnie had only been fired one time in his life. It was in high school and he had misread the schedule and showed up at the wrong time. He talked a lot about how disappointed his dad would be in him. He talked about his dad's reaction from long ago when he was fired from that job in high school. He clearly remembered his dad saying that he had never been fired in his life; he clearly remembered the disappointment on his dad's face. Donnie asked me not to tell anyone that he was fired. He was embarrassed and we agreed to tell people it just wasn't for him so he had quit.

Donnie had been on storm duty right before starting the new job. When you go on storm, you make a lot of money and our savings account had more money in it than it ever had. He could afford to be off work for a while and pursue other interests, and Donnie felt that God was clearly telling him to pursue other interests. I guess I wasn't that stressed about it because we really could afford to go without a paycheck for a while. Donnie was a good lineman and I had heard a phone conversation from his prior company telling him they would hire him back whenever he was ready. They hated to see him go. This brought me peace, knowing he could take some time off and return to the other company, even if he had to go back on the road again.

Over the next few days, I did what Donnie asked me to do. I told people, including our girls, that Donnie had quit his job to pursue other interests. I quickly found out that he just started telling everyone that he was fired and why and how unjust it was. This infuriated me as I felt it made me look like a liar.

Donnie began filling his time with people. He visited nursing homes, hospitals, and shut-ins from church. He also started visiting the people he had been in contact with four years ago during his manic time.

He began to work out with vengeance. He started taking supplements. He started hanging out at the school a lot, getting in summer workouts with the cross country and football teams. He lifted weights for hours every day. He began eating all natural again. He made the comment more than once that it was like he was tasting food for the first time. Everything tasted so good. All of this was bringing me back to four years ago, the hot sauce, the eating all natural. It was like déjà vu.

He began hanging out with our neighbors. I admit, I am friendly to the neighbors, but that is as far as it goes. There appears to be a lot of drinking down the street and I knew there was a drug history with the people who lived there. There is always a lot of foul language that I can hear from my yard, and again, I admit, I don't really want to associate with that. Donnie, however, thought God was telling him to spend time with them all of a sudden. He knew, because I had shared with him that I was concerned that things were starting over again. So most times, when he would go missing, he would eventually call and let me know where he had been, where he was at, and where he was going next, in detail.

He was missing a lot, just like four years ago, he would go off missing for hours at a time. This couldn't all be a coincidence. It was starting over, I knew, it was back.

CHAPTER 4

Tornado

I was certain that what happened four years ago was starting to happen again. However, it was different this time. The manic, the ideas, all of it was milder and would come and go. Four years ago, it just got increasingly worse. Was it the same thing? Maybe not. I remember my mom asking me, and I kept telling her, it is different this time.

By May, Donnie still wasn't working. The savings account was quickly dwindling. We had our first family vacation scheduled for June. We had already paid for lodging and saved up for the rest of the trip. But with Donnie not working, our vacation savings was going fast. I was pushing him to work, and he didn't really seem interested. He started to talk about all the ways he could stay home and pick up odd jobs to support us. I questioned him about insurance, if he didn't work, we would lose our insurance from his job and we had excellent coverage.

Shortly after my niece's graduation, there was a tornado in Oklahoma. Oklahoma City was devastated. This affected Donnie in a way that surprised me. We lived in Oklahoma for four years, so this seemed to make it personal for Donnie. Right away, he started making plans to go.

His story started out that he was going to pack up and go, and once he got there, he would get on a storm crew and work. He began packing. I quickly saw that he was unable to complete a task. He would start packing and quickly get sidetracked with some medial task, start on that, not be able to complete it, then go back to packing. He had hooked on to his flat-bed trailer. He went up to the attic and started taking everything he thought people might need. All of our camping supplies went on the trailer, power strips, winter coats, extension cords, boxes of nails, blankets, clothes from my garage sale pile.

I quickly began to panic. I was all for donating items, but a lot of the stuff he was packing to give away was stuff we used and would have to replace. When I tried to say something, the lectures started so I kept my mouth shut.

Donnie took a break from the packing. He went to visit people. I had no idea where he was going. When he returned, he told me where all he had been. He told me that he had gone to one of the deacons at church. He told me that he had told him what happened four years ago and how the church did not get involved. He told me he had visited our pastor and tried to get him to pick up and go to Oklahoma. He had visited an elderly couple from church and tried to get them to take their RV to Oklahoma. He visited Paul and asked him to think about letting Donnie take his side dump semi to haul wreckage. The list went on and on. He was frustrated by people not dropping everything and agreeing to follow him.

From what I gathered, he had told half the town about his going to Oklahoma. He had made me put it on Facebook, made me tell everyone he was going, if anyone wanted to go along. He asked for donated supplies or money and dogs. Donnie made me put on Facebook that he was taking our lab; he had seen on the news that they needed search dogs. He got no replies. This infuriated him.

I questioned him. I asked him if he was really going there to get line work or if he was going on a mission trip to donate his time. He then told me that he was planning to go out and start his own line business, his own storm crew. He started packing all of his tools. I had told his sister he was going. She told Donnie's dad. He called and Donnie asked him to go. He, of course, said no. This upset Donnie terribly. He told me that it hurt him that he was doing a good thing and all his dad did was question it. He told me that his dad hadn't even told him he was proud of him. Then he told me that his dad had never told him he was proud of him. Then he looked at me and said, "God is telling me I'm not supposed to go alone." Donnie spent the next several hours, sidetracked from his packing, trying to figure out who he could take.

I remember just sitting in the garage, watching all of this play out. I was confident he had no intention of getting on a storm crew. I was confident that showing up in the middle of tornado wreckage was not an opportune time to start a business. It wasn't possible: employees, equipment, insurance, it just wasn't possible. During his phone conversation with his dad, I heard him say that I was helping him pack, then he told his dad that Lori is all for this trip. Later, he would tell his mom the same thing on the phone. I had said nothing. I think he knew that what he was doing was…off. By telling people I was on board, it sounded less crazy.

Donnie's original plan was to be packed by 1:00 p.m. and head out. That time was quickly approaching. Donnie was throwing out names of people that might be able to go. He said God was telling him to take someone who was down on his luck, someone not working, and get them on a crew and help them make lots of money. I asked him if it was a good time to take someone with no experience as a grounds person. Storm crews moved fast. There would not be time teach someone as you went. He told me he would teach them all they needed to know on the drive. He finally told me that God was telling him to take one of his wrestlers he had coached over the years. Then he said, "What about Toby? I don't think he has a job right now." He left the half-full trailer to go find a passenger.

I sat, not moving, in the garage, just sat and stared at the trailer. Tommy had already talked to Donnie and had stopped by. I could tell by the way Tommy was avoiding eye contact with me that he knew it was happening again. I thought about all the storms Donnie had gone on. Big storms like the one in Oklahoma. I had gained some knowledge from his stories. I knew that he couldn't just show up out there and get on a crew. The crews would be established before they left. I knew that he couldn't get to damaged areas, ground zero, you might say. They don't let people just show up, not even people willing to help. I knew that the dogs they were asking for were trained search and rescue dogs. I had already questioned Donnie about all of these things. This brought him much irritation and he had an answer for everything. When I questioned him, he immediately questioned my faith.

Tommy asked me if it was happening again. I told him it was. I felt like the life was sucked out of me. There was nothing I could do, and this trip was going to cost him a lot. It was now about three o'clock. I had two people stop at my house to give money to Donnie for what he was doing. Then I had a phone call telling me that the church was going to donate a chainsaw for Donnie. I began to shake.

Donnie returned frustrated. No one was willing to pick up and leave their jobs to go to Oklahoma and he just couldn't understand it. I questioned him about people dropping money off at our house. He explained that the money would be donated to the victims. I asked him about the chainsaw. He said that was all a misunderstanding. He then moved his departure time to 6:00 p.m. I had somewhere to be at seven. By 6:45, he still wasn't packed, so when I left, I told him good-bye. He didn't plan to be there when I got back. He told me again that he wished he had a number for Toby.

I left, hoping and praying he would be gone when I got back at 8. I was going to a pre-K graduation and could hardly believe my eyes when I walked in. Toby. Right there in front of me, I walked right past him and said hi. I couldn't stop thinking how Donnie was looking for a way to get in contact with him, how Donnie said God had brought Toby to his mind. I knew I should tell Toby that Donnie was trying to get a hold of him, but I didn't.

At eight, I came home and the trailer was still in the driveway. It was full, not one more thing would fit on it. It reminded me a lot of the *Beverly Hillbillies*. I didn't tell Donnie that I saw Toby. He planned to leave. I wasn't happy about Donnie taking our dog, Bailey. She isn't a young dog, and she is not trained in search and rescue. She can sniff out a pheasant better than any, but that is not the same. I tried to tell Donnie this and he told me Bailey was his dog, and that if he came across anyone that needed her or some child that had lost a pet, he would be giving Bailey away. I was horrified. He told me he was also taking Rocky. This was our youngest daughter's dog, and Rocky is a great watchdog, but he doesn't do well around other dogs or chaos. I refused to let him take Lexi's dog.

I was sorry to see Bailey go, but quite honestly, I couldn't wait until Donnie left. Panic was seizing my chest. At 8:30, he left. He planned to drive all night; he wasn't tired he had told me. At ten o'clock, Donnie called me. He was still in town. He told me that I would never believe what had happened. As he was fueling up, he ran into Toby's cousin and Donnie told him where he was going. Of course, he didn't have to tell anyone. He had painted Oklahoma Relief on the walls of his trailer along with his cell phone number. Plus, he had already let most of the town know of his great deed. Toby's cousin said, "Hey, you should ask Toby to go, he isn't working right now."

And there you have it. Donnie had Toby's number and invited him to go. I had no way to justify this. Donnie said God had told him to take Toby. Then I walked in and Toby was right there. I ignored it, and sure enough, God got Donnie Toby's number. Here we go again. Am I the crazy one? Am I ignoring the fact that God might be directly communicating and leading Donnie? This was another déjà vu to things that happened four years ago.

Of course, Toby said yes. When Donnie called at ten, he told me they were finally leaving. He told me that Toby was leaving behind his girlfriend and three kids and could I please check on his girlfriend off and on as she didn't have a license. I told him that I didn't know this person and I wasn't going to. I had enough on my plate with him gone and I didn't need more.

Round 2 had started. It was in full swing. My panic was back. The only relief I had right now was Donnie being gone for a while. He would be gone at least a week, best I could figure. I prepared myself to get ready for what was coming. I was angry. Why? Why did this have to happen again? We had worked hard to pay off our debt, suffered with Donnie working on the road. I had every reason to question. I had every reason to be angry. I was angry at Donnie for not getting help. I was angry at God for letting it happen again.

CHAPTER 5

Toby

Donnie had coached Toby several years ago. Toby is a great kid who has made some bad choices. He had gotten himself in situations and he was still living the consequences of those situations. I knew Donnie's heart was in the right place. And I knew something else. There was no doubt in my mind that Toby would accept Christ on this trip. I remember telling Tommy and also Pastor Doug this. I was confident, if for no other reason, than this truly was where my nightmare four years ago left off and then picked up again. Good things were going to happen among all the chaos, and again, I was going to look like the crazy one.

I heard from Donnie often. The drive was amazing, according to him. He and Toby were digging into the Bible. No surprise. If I was so confident about Toby accepting Christ soon, why couldn't I be excited about it? I knew the answer. Even though good things would happen, my life was about to turn into a living hell again.

The travelers got to Oklahoma. They slept in the truck or on the trailer. Just as I predicted, there was no line job waiting for Donnie. There was no getting close to the devastation to help out. So Donnie and Toby drove around, trying to find people that had lost everything.

There were several stories Donnie would later tell. Stories of how they would pull into small cafes and people would see the Oklahoma Relief sign painted on the trailer. Because of this, people would give them money or free food. Donnie assured me he was coming out ahead, spending little. There was one story of a woman they came across who was crying and had lost everything. This is the woman who got all of the donated cash. Again, this was a great thing they had done; however, I felt no joy over it, only anger.

Then the call came. Donnie said he had great news. Toby had accepted Christ. Donnie felt his work was done there and they were going to head home. To ease his conscience, he threw in that they were going to "work" their way home. They were going to pick up odd jobs and make loads of money to fund the trip they had taken. I knew the decision Toby had made was beyond amazing, but I felt no joy.

The next call I got was to tell me they had gotten into the devastation area. I questioned Donnie, I knew they weren't letting people in, I had heard it on the news. The only thing I could get out of Donnie was that Bailey was going to go to work. I immediately asked him if he had lied and told people that Bailey was a trained search and rescue dog. Donnie admitted he had. I was furious. I asked him what if Bailey, being untrained and hyper, just got in the way and made things worse. This infuriated him and he hung up. About an hour later, he called again, saying they were on their way home. I have no idea what changed.

And that was that. They headed home. I knew they planned to stop in our hometown. That would buy me at least another couple days. Though I didn't agree with all that Donnie was doing, I was not happy that he would be returning home soon. I knew what lay ahead.

They made it to Donnie's mom's house. They stayed there a day or so. When they finally hit the road again, Donnie told Lexi he had a huge surprise. I knew what it was and it was literally huge. His mom had called and told me that he was bringing her horse. Donnie had left the trailer full of stuff at his mom's and brought their horse and horse trailer home instead. The reasoning for this was quite touching, or it would have been if I wasn't already preparing my heart to become hard.

You see, Toby had left, promising his kids he was going to make lots of money, maybe even enough money to buy them a pony. Toby didn't make a dime; however, Donnie made sure he brought his kids a pony. The horse would be kept at Toby's. Donnie's mom didn't sound real thrilled about it so I wasn't sure why she had agreed to it, but she had. We would need our trailer in a month as we planned to take it on vacation loaded with four-wheelers. Guess he hadn't thought of that.

When they finally returned from Oklahoma, Donnie was full of stories. And he was furious that Pastor Doug didn't ask about his adventure, didn't ask him to stand up in church and share all that had happened. I knew why but kept my mouth shut. I was relieved that I wouldn't have to listen to him stand up in front of the congregation and tell everyone how great he was, tell them of the great deeds he had done. It was then I noticed how important Donnie had become. How important he had become in his own mind. He was full of himself. A saying started that I would hear over and over. Not egbok this time. Nope, this time it was, "I don't mean to toot my own horn but…," and then he would go on to tell of his great deeds.

Before Donnie left, he had literally destroyed the garage. I had spent days cleaning it. The day he returned, he unloaded his truck in the garage and destroyed it once again. Out of everything he had taken, they accepted the nails. That was it. The relief system was so organized that you could not just drop off donations. A lot of what he brought home was still on the trailer at his mom's, but he had packed all he could in his truck.

Bailey returned in one piece. She had a great time with her master whom she adores. I was very grateful she returned to us. I was not so grateful to see Donnie. I noticed right away that his eyes were wild, just like four years ago. I could tell he was running on little sleep. And I knew the arguments would begin soon when I started to question him about going back to work.

CHAPTER 6

Back to Work

I was right. Donnie had no interest in going back to work. I didn't blame him for not wanting to go back on the road, but this was a consequence from quitting his job four years ago. With me pressuring him, he made some calls. He had lots of "contacts" as he liked to call them. He found out about a job an hour and a half from home. He called and they said they would take him. He agreed to do this to "bring his wife peace." He believed God would provide. I told him I doubted God was going to drop money into our bank account. In my mind, God had provided by bringing this job to Donnie.

He went to sign the books in Minneapolis. He was only gone for a day. He had to go back there later that week for his final paperwork. While he was in Minneapolis, he called me often. Everything he saw, he thought was a sign. That would be the next thing that he would get hung up on, signs from God. He said he didn't believe in coincidence any more, everything was a sign from God.

For example, at one point when he was in Minneapolis that day, he called very excited. He had seen a sign that read CJ construction or something on that order. The reason for his excitement was because God had brought him past that sign. CJ was a young boy that Donnie had met when he was in high school. Donnie, myself, and our friend Lisa had gone for a week to be counselors at a camp for abused children. CJ was Donnie's camper. He was immediately convinced that God had driven him by this sign to tell him he needed to help abused children in some way. Donnie would go as far as trying to contact the people who ran the camp years ago. Donnie also believed that it was very possible that this CJ was the same CJ that had been his camper all those years ago.

Donnie asked me to make the three-hour trip with him next time. I agreed to avoid angering him. It was a long day to say the least. He had to drive me past the sign that read CJ. We went right to it. It was very out of the way. I asked him how he had found it. He said that he had gotten lost and ended up there because God needed him to see it. I looked at the sign. I saw a C but no J. I questioned Donnie. He agreed that the sign did not say CJ. He said he was lacking sleep and must have misread the sign.

It was a long drawn-out day. We literally waited on paperwork for eight hours. During that time, Donnie looked for contacts. People he needed to touch base with. He was bound and determined to start his own line company. This job he had lined up was simply to keep us going until he got his own company running. I knew it wouldn't happen, not with his thinking so unclear, but at least he was willing to work.

I believe in Donnie, when he is Donnie. If he was trying to start a company any other time, I believed he could do it, but not now. He wasn't thinking clearly. He wanted to drop everything and start a company. He would become angry when I would mention that most people starting a company did it gradually and kept working while they got the new company started. This is when he told me that he had talked to a guy who started a company on credit cards alone. I told him I thought we were done with credit cards. He said that he had been wrong about that. He said he was willing to be a "slave to the bank" if that is what it took to start his company.

Donnie's goals for the company were to take every down-and-outer he knew and give them a job. I didn't believe a company could run this way, especially not a line company dealing with electricity. Donnie was an excellent lineman and also a good teacher. But I knew you had to have experienced people on board with you. When I talked to Donnie about this, he told me his brother was going to start the company with him. His brother is also a lineman. He said they had talked about starting the company four years ago and now his brother was considering it again. I hadn't heard anything about the company since Donnie's last manic episode and I had never heard his brother say anything about it, so I wasn't convinced that he was on board.

Sitting in the parking lot waiting, two Hispanic men on motorcycles pulled in. They were dressed in skinny jeans and leather. Donnie immediately went to talk to them. He came back smiling, not able to believe his luck. He had gotten their number. They were tree trimmers, and Donnie was going to hire them once his company was up and running. They had told him how good they were at their jobs. I questioned him and said if they were that good, why they were here trying to find work. This brought about a lecture, and I was called a doubting Thomas.

Bored with waiting, we took several breaks to drive around. At one point, Donnie pulled into a bar. It was three o'clock in the afternoon. I asked what we were doing there. Donnie said he wanted to go in and have a drink. I told him I didn't want to. I'm not a drinker and especially not at three in the afternoon. Donnie isn't a drinker either, or he wasn't, I guess. He left me in the truck to wait while he went for a drink. When he came out, I told him I was going to drive and he became very angry. So he drove and I sat with tears in my eyes.

We returned home, and the following Sunday night, Donnie would leave for his new job and return home on the weekends. He lined up borrowing a camper from Paul. There was a beautiful city park there and camping would be cheap. I wasn't convinced that Paul wanted to lend the camper out. He and his kids used it quite a bit during the summer. Donnie talked him in to leaving the camper at the park and Paul and his kids could use it there on the weekends and Donnie would use it during the week. That is the story Donnie told me anyway. I never discussed it with Paul, but I had a feeling Donnie was hearing what he wanted to hear.

Later when Donnie returned and we were outside loading the camper,

I looked down the street. A block away, walking toward us was Julio!

CHAPTER 7

Julio Returns

Since Julio went to college, and even since he graduated, we saw him little. So I was thrilled to look down the street and see him coming for a visit. No matter that Julio still continued to make bad choices. I loved him unconditionally and seeing him always made me smile. It was a gentle reminder from God that I had followed what He had put before me.

Julio was one of the people that Donnie wanted to make contact with. Julio was one that Donnie felt he had let down four years ago. As we were catching up, I quickly noticed Donnie's interest in Julio. After Donnie's last "episode," he had showed little interest in Julio and at times would seem irritated when he was around. I thought this was probably part of the reason we rarely saw Julio, he felt it, I'm sure.

I watched Julio soak up the attention from Donnie. He began to glow and my heart began to ache for him. I knew the reason for the attention. Donnie was manic, and like before, he had extreme interest in Julio and helping him. Julio hadn't been able to find steady work. He was down and frustrated. Donnie began the promises. He asked Julio to move with him to his next job. Donnie was sure God had brought Julio at that exact moment, just hours before Donnie pulled out with the camper.

Of course, Julio began to get excited. He felt it was going to be his new beginning. He was promised he would find work. He was promised a fresh start. And for now, he had Donnie's attention. Attention he craved. He didn't hesitate when Donnie invited him along.

After Julio left, I talked to Donnie about his lack of interest in Julio after his depression. He felt bad about it and said he wanted to make it up to him. I told Donnie I had a confession to make. This past Christmas, Julio had asked to come join us for the holiday as he was going to be alone. I knew Donnie didn't want him around. So I ignored his message he had sent me and left him sitting alone. This had broken my heart, but I was trying to help Donnie enjoy the holidays, and I knew if Julio was there, Donnie would feel agitated. When I told Donnie this, he cried right along with me.

I told Donnie then that I felt God had brought Julio into our lives. We had helped Julio, spent thousands without giving it a second thought. I told Donnie that I believed that is why God had blessed us with paying off all of our credit cards. Donnie seemed to agree with me.

Even though Donnie was manic, even though I knew this was the reason for the sudden attention Julio was getting from him, I was all for helping Julio. I have always been willing to do whatever we could for this young man. Life had dealt him a raw hand and it hurt my heart.

Donnie and Julio left late that night. They went to the campsite in their new town. It was only an hour and a half away. I knew Donnie didn't want to be away from home again, and I was scared to death that he would not keep this job. We had to have income. For this reason, I agreed to visit Donnie every week with Lexi. Each week, we planned to drive and stay for three or four days to visit. I wasn't happy about this, but it was my only option if I wanted him to keep working. It was hard keeping everything going at home, inside and outside the house, by myself. I didn't feel I could keep up if I was gone four days out of every week.

Donnie would be working six days a week and I didn't visit the first week. By the second week, Donnie had made yet another "contact" and found a different place to stay. It would be even cheaper than the camp grounds and it was on a ranch. The little apartment that they would move into was attached to a riding arena, and Donnie was beyond excited. He loved horses.

I wanted Donnie to be content so I was happy for him. However, this ranch was at least ten miles from town. Julio had no license and so this made finding a job impossible. Donnie was only thinking of himself.

Donnie and I weren't getting along on the phone. He seemed to like his job, but his mania seemed to be growing. He openly shared at work that he was trying to start his own company. He told me a lot of the crew was interested in working for him once he got it started. I didn't believe him.

One evening, Donnie called me and the call was not going well. We were fighting by the end of it. I told him I was not going to bring Lexi for a visit when he was acting the way he was. This angered him further. He told me to come the next day. He said Julio would be starting a job. Donnie planned to drop him off when he went to work, but Julio had no way of getting back to the ranch after work. He told me to come and bring the bike for Julio. He told me where he would be working and what time he would get off. I needed to be there by 4:00 p.m. I was so angry at Donnie that I told him I would come, but I would be gone before he got off work. I did not want to see him.

I went and arrived when I was supposed to. I found the place of Julio's employment. I waited in the parking lot. At 4:00, the factory started to empty. Within fifteen minutes, I was the only one left in the parking lot. I kept waiting, thinking that Julio was doing paperwork or something. Finally, I called him. Julio told me he did not have a job. He told me Donnie dropped him off for an interview, but the factory was not hiring at the time. Julio had walked all the way back to the ranch; it had taken him hours in the heat. Donnie had known it was only for an interview the night before. He had lied. I was furious. I got directions to the new bachelor pad, delivered the bike, visited with Julio briefly, and left. I was angered to tears by the deception that had happened, by what my miserable life had become.

I was about halfway home when Donnie called. He was chipper and excited. He asked where I was. I told him. I quickly realized Donnie thought I was on my way to see him, not on my way home. I told him I was headed home. He was upset, crying, I think. I felt bad. He missed me and wanted to see me. Why did he have to lie? I felt horrible for leaving. He called me back later and said that he and Julio were headed to the casino for supper and that he forgave me. That was a big thing for him these days. He knew the Bible said to forgive so he forgave everything, yet he never forgot.

Later that week, our friend Denny called and asked me if I knew that Donnie was planning to buy houses where he was living. I told him I knew nothing about it. Denny had talked to Donnie and Donnie had told him he was going to buy two or three rundown houses so Julio could fix them up. Then they would rent them out or sell them. Later, Donnie would tell me this, much later.

The next week, I took Lexi to visit her dad. It was a rough few days. I was miserable. Donnie's manic behavior wore on my nerves. We fought most of the weekend. Our vacation was coming up and Donnie was insisting we go and put it all on credit card. He sat me down and told me he had changed the plan for vacation. His new plan was leaving on the same day, driving nine hours to Arizona to visit his aunt and uncle. He told me his uncle was in very poor health. We would stay one day there, then drive to Colorado, and make it there in one day. We would only waste two days of our cabin stay that was already paid for.

I was furious. When we had started planning our vacation, I tried very hard to get Donnie to go to Arizona for the whole trip. Our whole family would have loved to visit his aunt and uncle. He did not want to go to Arizona in the summer; he said it was too hot. We had finally decided on Colorado. Donnie had told Taylor to plan the trip once the lodging was set up. She had a very detailed itinerary. She was incredibly upset when she heard of the changes Donnie wanted to make. She called Donnie's mom and asked the condition of Donnie's uncle. His mom said he was doing well, not on his death bed by any means. Taylor also asked her about the length of the drive. Could it be done in nine hours? His mom said it would take us over twenty-four hours straight through. Donnie and Taylor began to fight on the phone. Donnie finally gave in but was very angry about it. He began throwing out that he was the head of the household and he got no respect. I remembered our meeting and Pastor Doug asking Donnie about being the head of the house, the leader. Donnie became obsessed with this and totally took it out of context with what Pastor had meant.

Another irritation of that trip was cage fighting. Julio wanted to compete again. Wrestling was done for him, so he wanted to cage fight. Donnie was trying to plan a fight for him while we were there. That meant that Lexi and I would be sitting alone in the bachelor pad. I didn't love the bachelor pad; it was dirty and not very private. There were no TV channels that came in, and I threatened to leave if they were going to be gone to a cage fight. The cage fight fell through, but that is when Donnie announced that he was going to begin training. He was dead set on cage fighting. This went in one ear and out the other. Donnie had so many ideas going through his head and he couldn't complete a task to save his life. I noticed that while Donnie was on the phone, trying to set up the fight that he referred to Julio as his son. Everywhere we went, Donnie introduced him as his son. Julio glowed; I just wished there was some way I could protect him.

I was relieved for Donnie to go to work the next day. Julio, Lexi, and I went to a park. While Lexi played, Julio asked me some questions. First, he asked if I had any concerns about Donnie gambling. I told him I did not. Then he asked me if I had any concerns about Donnie with other women. Again, I told him I did not. I had always trusted Donnie, even when he was on the road. Julio then told me that Donnie had taken him to the casino. Donnie had played blackjack for hours. Julio got so tired of waiting that he went to the truck and slept in the bed of it. Donnie gambled until just a few hours before he had to be at work. Julio also told me that Donnie had visited with pretty girls. Donnie had told Julio to keep this between the two of them. Julio said Donnie had won at the blackjack tables and that he was very good.

I talked to Julio a little about Donnie and his behaviors. I explained that I thought he was bipolar. Julio told me he had seen the behavior and that a lot of things didn't make sense. Julio got tears in his eyes as he told me he felt that this was why Donnie had a sudden interest in him again. He knew, and my heart broke for him.

CHAPTER 8

Pastor Exasperation

Everyone knows about pastor appreciation month. Well, here at our house, we blessed ours with pastor exasperation month. We had had the initial meeting with Pastor. I was keeping him updated on things, and I'm pretty sure Donnie had been in his office more than once.

Donnie and I began fighting worse and worse. He was demanding I come to where he was working more and more. It was a constant fight with Lexi making her go. I didn't want to go either, but I wanted to keep him working. Donnie couldn't understand why I couldn't just go and stay for the summer.

Every other week when we went to visit, we would stay at the casino hotel instead of the ranch. I hated staying at the ranch, and Lexi seemed to be in the way there. The hotel had a pool where Lexi and I could at least fill a few hours each day. But when we did stay at the hotel, Donnie would get off work, we would eat, and then Donnie would ask Lexi if she wanted to go to the play area. This was a day care service the hotel provided. Then he and I would walk around outside and "spend time together." This was fine once in a while, but it happened every night we were there. Donnie was always on my case that he wasn't seeing Lexi enough, then he would put her in the day care. I was frustrated.

Bedtime would come and I would tuck Lexi in and get ready for bed. Donnie would then get ready to go gamble. He would be in the casino until one, two, or even sometimes three in the morning. He would sleep a few hours, then get up and leave for work. One morning I woke to find five hundred dollars lying on the hotel TV stand. Donnie was happy about how good he was at blackjack. We needed the money, especially staying in the hotel every other week. I didn't say anything to him. I knew it would agitate him and it was pointless. I couldn't stop him. He was at the casino every night whether I was there or not.

I had let Pastor Doug know that our fighting was about to come to a head. I told him I wanted Donnie out. I couldn't do it anymore. I knew if I didn't get away from him soon that I would hate him. Pastor advised me to wait through the weekend. He told me that if we could get Donnie to get some help, it wouldn't happen over Memorial Day weekend, and he might change his mind by the time anything was open. I agreed that he was right.

My temper, however, did not agree and got the best of me. Over the long weekend, when he was home, things just kept escalating. I was about to snap, and eventually, I did. One night, Donnie had taken Lexi on a four-wheeler ride. This took place at around ten. I told him it was her bedtime. He became angry and said that she was his daughter and he could make decisions about her. By midnight, I was frantic. Where could they have gone? I called and called. No answer. Finally, Taylor called and got through. They had been out on a country bridge looking at the stars. On their way back to town, they had been pulled over for a taillight out.

I was furious when they got back. I didn't trust Donnie. I didn't trust his judgment where Lexi was concerned and I didn't trust his driving. He had become careless, reckless, and he hadn't been sleeping. He had a dorm room–size refrigerator in the garage, and it was well stocked with beer and liquor. He drank when he wanted, it didn't matter the time of day. He was doing a lot of drinking and he wasn't afraid to get behind the wheel and drive.

Donnie had already told Lexi they were going to have a sleepover in our shed. Donnie had destroyed our shed; it was full and unorganized. Nothing would fit in there, and there was definitely no place to sleep. I told Lexi to go to bed. I knew it would take Donnie hours before he created a nook for them to lie in, and I also was afraid he would go out wandering in the night since that is what he did. If Lexi woke and he wasn't there, she would be frightened.

Donnie and I began to fight in front of Lexi, both of us telling her something different. I finally got Lexi to bed and Donnie left outraged. I didn't know where he was going and I didn't care. Lexi was upset, and I knew it was time she and I had a talk.

The next day, I did visit with Lexi. Lexi told me that she knew it wasn't right for a daddy to keep a little girl out so late, even if they were having fun. She also didn't really want to have a sleepover in the shed. She was tired and wanted to go to bed but had been afraid to tell her dad no. Lexi told me she knew something wasn't right with her dad, he wasn't acting right. And she knew I would be worried with her gone so long. Lexi is wise beyond her years, and she seemed to understand. I told her I didn't want to scare her but that she was always to let me know where she was going and not to go anywhere without my permission. I also told her if her dad was trying to force her into doing things she didn't want to do or didn't feel safe doing, it was okay to say no. I told her if he became angry that I would step in and take the blame.

Donnie was furious at me the next day. According to him, I had ruined a perfect father-daughter fun night. Our arguing grew until I lost it. I told him he either get some help or get out. As our fighting intensified, he called Pastor Doug. I told him to stop bothering Pastor. I knew Doug was exhausted by us and had no clue how to help. I knew there was nothing he or anybody else could do. I was ashamed of myself for losing control in front of my girls. They heard it all.

Pastor came and sat. We went round and round and got nowhere. I wanted Donnie out. He said everything was my fault. Tommy happened to call and Donnie told him and Beth to come over. I began to calm down once Beth was there and we all were able to talk Donnie into at least going to the ER here in town.

It was sad, watching Donnie, spinning his wheels, conversations going nowhere, trying to justify everything and having it all make sense in his mind and sounding ridiculous to the rest of us. Sometimes, I would see a look on his face that he was confused and that things didn't sound right even to him. For a split second, this would make me pity him. Tommy told him to go to the ER to give me peace, to calm me down. Tommy thought this the best way. Donnie seemed to think everything was my fault, so Tommy put the blame on me to get Donnie to go. I didn't care; whatever worked.

We went. The doctor asked why we were there. It took Donnie half an hour to tell what was going on. He told the doctor about the ideas, about God working through him four years ago, and how he had gone his own way, how God had punished him. He told her God was giving him a second chance to do it right.

Then the doctor looked at me and my answer took about twenty seconds. Four years ago, he had three months of manic behavior and then two months of depression. He is now in a manic mode again. The doctor was so good. She listened and chose her words carefully. She told Donnie that having a conversation with him reminded her of trying to have a conversation with her uncle who was bipolar. She suggested he try a medication called Abilify. She said it would take the edge off his manic behavior, slow down the thoughts. Donnie agreed to it to bring his wife peace. I told him if he took the meds, he could stay. Maybe this would help. The doctor also suggested we make an appointment with a psychiatrist.

My frustration grew. As I tried to fill the prescription, I quickly learned that even with our awesome insurance, the medication would cost $689 a month. I began to cry in the drugstore. I begged and told them we had to have it. They gave me some numbers to call and try to get assistance.

With our great insurance, there was no assistance. How did people ever get help? I couldn't commit him unless he was going to hurt himself or someone else. I couldn't even get the meds he had finally agreed to take.

My frustration grew more as I tried to make a psychiatry appointment. I called everywhere in the area. The soonest I could get an appointment was July. Even if Donnie was agreeing to go now, he might not agree to go in three months. And how much worse could things get in that amount of time?

I began to scour through Donnie's information from work. I called the insurance company and begged. They gave me a number and I found out that I could get a three month supply for $29. Thank you, God. It would take about three weeks to get here, but it was coming. Hopefully by then, he would still be willing to take it.

My hands constantly shook from here on out. I was so strung out. My hands didn't stop shaking, not ever. I had constant panic attacks. I quickly forgot about God helping me with the medication. I became furious with God. Why wouldn't He help me? No one else could, only God. I knew it, everybody knew it. There was nothing anyone could do, and no matter how much I begged and pleaded, I felt I was on my own. Finally, I stopped praying. It had done me no good. I was alone. Friends rallied around me, but they couldn't help me. Nobody could except God, and He wouldn't.

CHAPTER 9

Vacation

Vacation time had arrived. Our family had never taken a family vacation before. We were excited, yet the girls and I were dreading the trip because of Donnie's behavior. The plan was to take the truck, loaded, and whatever needed to go on the trailer would be put in the horse trailer until we reached our hometown. Then we would switch out trailers and be on our way. One pickup and six passengers, Taylor's boyfriend Ethan is part of the family, and he was going along with us.

Packing of course was taking forever. We had an exact departure time. Everyone was packed except Donnie. He was packing anything anyone might ever need. He took me with him to the hardware store. We went down every aisle, and he filled a cart. Anything we could possibly need and lots of stuff we didn't. We spent $300 at that store. He kept saying, "Better to have and not need than need and not have." Over and over, he said this. He kept saying he wished he had a concealed weapon permit. You never know about people, bears, cougars, mountain lions. Paranoia had set in again.

Soon, I noticed Donnie on the phone with his mom. He was asking her about baby calves. He told her he could get some newborn bull calves that were going to be killed from a dairy here. He had the trailer, and if she was interested, he would pick some up. She said yes, two or three only, and told him it could be done another time if we needed to get on the road. Donnie left for the dairy. We were planning to leave very early the next morning. We had to stop along the way to pick up Julio. Julio had found work with a friend and had left with me on one of my visits to Donnie. We would pick him up on our way and he would stay with Donnie's mom and stepdad. Donnie's stepdad had a construction company and had agreed to hire Julio. This would make most of the first leg of our trip very crowded.

Donnie returned from the dairy with four calves. One was half dead. The calves had scours and Donnie stayed up most of the night pouring all-natural things down their throats. I'm not sure what all he tried: Gatorade, water, peroxide. And everything he put in multiplied as it went straight through. The trailer was a smelly mess and part of our luggage was back there. Taylor and I quickly switched out the luggage and only Donnie's suitcase ended up riding with the calves.

It is a five-hour drive to our hometown. We picked up Julio and scrunched in. Julio had asked to join us on the vacation. He said he wanted to cage fight while in Colorado. I told him I was not going to be running him around to cage fights on vacation and that I was sorry, but it was too crowded and our cabin only slept six. I felt bad. Donnie called him son and he wasn't even invited on the vacation. Donnie had already asked to take him along, and I had told him it just wouldn't work. I didn't feel we could pay his way when we really couldn't afford the trip to begin with and we really didn't have room.

The drive took many stops to keep the calves alive. I heard Donnie call the guy from the dairy, bragging that the calf they said wouldn't make it was still alive. By the looks of the calf, it was struggling to hang on. To me, it looked like it was suffering terribly. All of the passengers were very frustrated. We were already behind schedule. Our five-hour drive to our hometown took eight. Then we had to switch out trailers and load four-wheelers.

Finally, the calves were dropped off, four-wheelers loaded, and we were on the road. Ethan became the navigator and Donnie could not focus enough to even head the right direction. He missed turn after turn even with the GPS, and soon, Ethan had to tell Donnie every single move. Donnie's driving had changed drastically. Normally, he is a very cautious driver, but he had become reckless. He was also driving very fast.

The drive to our destination was excruciating. We made many stops. Not just gas and food stops. Donnie would all of a sudden announce he needed out of the vehicle right now and we would stop. Each stop, for whatever reason, took at least an hour. Donnie had to talk to every person he saw. I am not exaggerating when I say every person. He struck up a conversation with kids, women, men, everybody. We started to notice that every person Donnie talked to heard the same story. My humble husband had become very arrogant.

He told everybody about his hard life growing up, his absentee father, how he was labeled as a child in school. He told everyone that he was a wrestling coach (he hadn't coached for three years), that he was a lineman by trade, he even told people he had recently been training horses. I'm assuming this came from petting the horses on the ranch where he was staying. He told everyone he was starting his own business. He got business cards and wrote down numbers of "contacts." He wrote numbers on his clothing, on his skin, on napkins, scraps of paper, maps, coolers, everywhere, numbers of people we would never see again.

He also told everyone he saw that he was Native American. Donnie had recently found out that his great-grandfather was at least half Native American, possibly full. My heart was becoming hard, and the way I saw it, that gave Donnie about an ounce of Native American blood. Donnie became obsessed when he started visiting the casino regularly. He would talk to the Native Americans there and tell his story and then hear theirs. He wanted to help all of them. Later, on this trip, he would search out the Native Americans in the area and also start wearing a bear claw around his neck.

One of Donnie's new obsessions was thrift stores, Goodwill, and pawn shops. He couldn't drive past one without going in. According to Donnie, God would tell him how many items he had to buy. For example, in one store, Donnie had found two items to purchase. We had gone through the whole store and couldn't leave because God had told him to buy three things. He had to find something else to buy. We had to go in several of these on our vacation, and this would continue for the next several months. The girls and I would receive many gifts that we did not need, want, or like from thrift stores.

The drive was exhausting and sickening. Donnie had lost interest in hygiene. He was not showering or using deodorant. He had let his beard go and he started to chew and smoke. He reeked. He had chewing tobacco and food in his beard. The air conditioner wasn't working well in the already crowded truck, and when we started to complain about him not bathing or using deodorant, he began to wipe himself down with baking soda and air fresheners. He had become disgusting. I cannot imagine the horror for Taylor, having Ethan along. I was sure she had told him of the situation, and he had to see it, but still, it had to be humiliating.

Finally, a whole day late, we arrived at our cabin. It was beautiful and serene. It should have been a great relaxing time, but right away, things became even worse.

CHAPTER 10

Wolves

One of our favorite parts of our vacation was a wolf refuge we visited. All three of our girls got to choose something they wanted to do on vacation and an animal refuge was hands down Lexi's first choice. The original plan was to go to one on the way that had all kinds of animals. Due to our delayed start and not being able to stay on course or follow the planned-out route, we weren't able to go. Lexi was very disappointed so we began to search for another refuge.

We found one not far from where we were staying. This one was just for wolves. We went there, not realizing we needed an appointment, but the man in charge said he would go ahead and give us a tour. During the whole tour, Donnie was sharing all of his thoughts, his business he wanted to start, his horse training and other "animal" experiences, and mostly he was sharing about his Native American heritage. Exhausting and embarrassing are the only words I can think of to describe it. The man giving us the tour was kind and didn't seem to notice.

Each wolf was rescued. Some were domesticated and some abused. It was very interesting and we could get right in the cage with most of the wolves. The man giving the tour had a story about each one. He also shared that his first wolf, which had passed away, was able to detect cancer in people. The stories were captivating, and we soon forgot about our troubles.

The man explained the healing of the wolves, the sense they had. He explained that if there is something wrong in your body, the wolves can usually detect it and try to do lots of licking in that area. Licking to them is healing. This will sound bizarre, I know, but the kids and I soon noticed that every cage we went in, the wolves immediately went to Donnie and they would start licking his head. The wolves were huge, and if Donnie didn't kneel down, they would put their paws on his shoulders to reach his head. After hearing the man explain how the wolves could detect something wrong in the body and that they would lick that area, well, I already knew something was wrong in Donnie's head, bipolar, I believed, and I was convinced the wolves had picked up on it.

Our visit ended with Donnie asking how he could help. Donnie asked if they had a need for big poles as he had access to throw-away power line poles and he would be happy to bring them all the way to Colorado. The man shared that there is always a need for supplies like that for enclosures. He said the main need was fresh meat. Donnie believed it was his duty to help, and he spent the rest of the vacation wanting to go prairie dog hunting and take all the meat to the wolf refuge. He never got around to it.

CHAPTER 11

Bad to Worse

Something I began to learn was, just when I thought things couldn't get worse, they could. Donnie became frustrated that we weren't spending our vacation on an Indian refuge, that he wasn't hunting to provide food for the wolves, frustrated about everything. He was very irritable. Any time we were ready to leave the cabin, we had to wait, wait, and wait. Most times, we waited an hour or more. He would have to organize the cab and bed of the truck. He would be off, wandering; he was never ready.

We spent three days riding the four-wheelers we had brought along. This was a great time for the most part.

Donnie, in his paranoia, would become irritable. Certain things were horrifying to him, yet he told Lexi she didn't have to wear a helmet. I remember Taylor coming to me upset and saying that she, Kaylee, and Ethan were going to refuse to ride if Lexi didn't wear a helmet. It made no sense, Donnie's paranoia, yet he was not going to make her wear a helmet. The refusing to ride brought about victory in this situation.

On one ride, we came across junk that people had used for target practice. All along the way, Donnie would stop to collect garbage to throw away later. It was his duty. We came across an old hot tub cover, full of bullet holes; Donnie instantly wanted it. Yes, one man's garbage was Donnie's treasure. Donnie had begun to talk a lot about his growing-up days, about his mom and how she raised two kids on her own and worked many jobs. He talked a lot about how they had to go without. He remembered one time losing a shoe and how it affected his whole family as his mom had to find the money to buy a new pair. This is how he would justify his hoarding. When you do without, everything is treasure.

Well, the hot tub lid, according to Donnie, could be attached to our truck to make us aerodynamic on the way home. I made sure Ethan and Taylor's four-wheeler was in the front and that we took a different route back. The hot tub lid was forgotten.

Also on our ride, we drove past an old car. I can't tell you the make or model of the car. It was old and a hatchback. According to Donnie, he had always wanted one, and they had only made so many in the United States. So of course, we had to stop and ask about the car since it was for sale. We quickly found that the car didn't run and that they were asking a thousand dollars for it. Donnie wanted it. I said no and we left. What were we going to do with a car that wouldn't run, in Colorado? Not to mention we couldn't afford it.

Donnie became obsessed with getting the car. I knew that part of the obsession was helping the man who was selling it. He had major medical problems and, by the looks of things, little money. We began to fight about the car. He kept throwing in my face that he was the leader of our family, and if he wanted the car, he was getting it. He said he needed it to drive back and forth to work, said he could use it for his business.

He became very irritable over this and I would not back down. We were putting our whole trip and everything else on credit cards and we couldn't afford it. Our fighting became terrible. What I am about to tell you I am not proud of. In fact, I'm ashamed. At one point during our fighting, I lost it. I began to use terrible profanity at Donnie, words I hate hearing and words I never say. I'm not sure I had ever said those words in my life. I was just so frustrated and tired. We had already talked at this point about a divorce, and I told him if he spent the money on that car, then I was done. He threatened me then, for the first time, that if I walked, he would make sure he took Lexi from me. This caused me to call him a bipolar freak. I told him if he ever tried that, I would make sure the whole world knew he was bipolar and had no business taking care of a child. Then, Donnie said something to me that I will never forget. With a bottled-up, controlled rage, he said, "You pushed me into depression once before and I'm never going back to that place." Then he told me I was a foolish woman.

Donnie left the room and I went to bed. He went out and told Taylor about the profanity I had used against him, that I had asked for a divorce, and that I was going to take Lexi from him. Taylor was furious and told her dad how embarrassed she was by all of this with Ethan there. Then she told her dad that she hated him and me. Donnie couldn't wait to get back to the room. His words were, "Taylor told me she hates me and she hates you too." Then he told me he was leaving. He spent the next two or three hours "packing." Then he left. The next morning when I got up, the whole living room of the cabin had his stuff scattered all over it. He had made piles, piles of clothes, piles of receipts and contacts, piles of magazines, piles of personal items. It was all there, but Donnie wasn't. His Abilify was on the counter. I knew exactly how many should be gone: twenty. There should only be eight pills left. I dumped the bottle into my hand and counted. There were only eight pills missing. I had asked him daily if he had taken his medicine and he had lied.

He was gone for a long time. He had taken the truck. I was furious about this. There were a lot of wildfires that summer and you could smell the smoke all the time. We were in the middle of nowhere, and I didn't appreciate being left there with no way out. I went up and explained to the kids what had happened the night before. I apologized and explained that I was strung out and exhausted. Soon, Donnie returned, no sleep, yet looking surprisingly refreshed.

He announced that he was going to talk to the man about the car. He had already gone to do this but couldn't find it. He needed Ethan to show him how to get there and then he was going to go and barter. Bartering was another one of Donnie's new obsessions. Why should anybody ever have to pay for anything when you could trade this for that? In fact, he felt he could run his business on bartering. He said that if he could get the guy to give the car to him, to trade something for it, then he would get it. If not, then God was shutting that door. My worries were over. Donnie is the only person I knew who would give away a car.

Donnie was also thinking about sending us home and staying in Colorado to get line work. They were desperate for workers with all the fires and damage. This was his way to justify getting the car. His plan was to send us home and keep a four-wheeler with him. He would drive that until the car was running. He would be helping work on the car. I asked him how he would finally get home. He said his plan was to load the four-wheeler on top of the car to travel home. I remember just looking at him. He was serious, not joking at all.

Donnie wanted us to wait at the bottom of the hill while he went to talk to the man about the car. Kaylee went with him to keep him on task. Donnie made her stay in the truck while he bartered; he said it was a man's conversation that she didn't need to hear. This really made me wonder what he was bartering with, but I will never know. They returned in half an hour with no car. God had "shut the door," yet Donnie would not get the car out of his head the rest of the trip.

CHAPTER 12

Heading Home

The trip home was even worse than the ride there. Lexi had talked her dad out of staying and working in Colorado. Honestly, I would have been relieved if he would have stayed. Ideas seemed to be coming faster and faster into Donnie's head. And the ideas seemed to be getting more and more bizarre. And none of the ideas included holding down a full-time job.

Kaylee had been saving up and looking for a car. Her dad talked her into looking while we were on vacation. Colorado doesn't put salt on their roads so rust on vehicles is usually minimal. She ended up finding a car so Ethan, Taylor, and

Kaylee decided to take a different route home than us. This would get them there at least a day earlier as we still had to stop in our hometown and drop off the borrowed four-wheelers and pick up some stuff Donnie had left at his mom's.

Right away, when we were pulling onto the interstate, we passed a hitchhiker. Donnie said he was going back for him. I told him no. This agitated him and the lectures began. He said I was judging the person by how they looked and were dressed, shabby and dirty. Maybe he was right, but I wouldn't have let him pick up anybody with Lexi in the vehicle with us. The sermons began. I was getting preached at a lot lately. Not just little reprimands, full-blown sermons from somebody who seemed to think they were God in the flesh.

Donnie noticed we were having tire problems. The rear tires both looked pretty thin, and we searched towns along the way to find a place to replace them. The drive was taking forever. Yes, most people would have done this before leaving for vacation, especially pulling a trailer. Anyway, it was Saturday afternoon and we weren't having much luck. He didn't really think we could make it to our hometown without replacing them.

As we were driving, Donnie put Lexi on the phone. He had her call his dad, sisters, and brothers, an ex-brother-in-law, his grandma, and I don't even know who else. He was having her tell everyone we were coming to town and to meet us at a certain time so he could see everyone. I became frustrated. I wanted to make a drop-off and leave. I had had enough of being around Donnie and I wasn't looking forward to everyone else questioning me later about his odd behavior. I guess God worked it out for me. The belt in one of our tires broke and we were stranded in the middle of nowhere. It took Donnie over four hours to change the tire to the spare. That put us into a hotel for the night.

Sunday was spent searching for a place to replace the tires. For this reason, we did not have time to face all the people Donnie had called. We ended up making the drop-offs we needed too and headed home. Julio decided to stay there and continue working.

As Donnie went out to make sure everything was tied down on the trailer, his mom said something about Donnie smoking. I think she suspected he was, Lexi had said a few things that made her think so and you could smell it on him. Lexi was upset about her dad smoking and constantly begged him to stop. Donnie's mom made the comment when he was on his way out the door. I, without thinking, said, "It's too late." Donnie must have caught that. When he came back in, his mom was crying, and when he asked her why, she told him she had found out about his smoking. Her dad and late husband had suffered with emphysema and it terrified her that Donnie had picked up this habit.

We all headed out the door and Donnie let me have it, verbally. He didn't care who heard, he didn't care that Lexi was standing there. He chewed me out in front of everyone, screaming at me and looking beyond angry. It was one of those times that I felt Donnie would have hit me if he hadn't had an audience.

I kept my mouth shut and fought the tears. Donnie's mom yelled for him to stop. This just enraged him more. I wasn't about to tell him Lexi was the one who brought the whole thing up so I took it. Donnie screamed at me to tell all of them about my bad habit. "Why don't you tell them about your bad habit, do you think you're perfect?" I looked at everybody and through my tears confessed my sin. Yep, I drink one Diet Coke a day. I knew that is what Donnie was talking about. He was on my case all the time about my drinking the Diet Coke, the poison it contained. After all, tobacco was just a leaf, an all-natural leaf, so it wasn't hurting Donnie at all, according to him.

His mom felt bad and responsible for me getting chewed out. I told her not to worry, it wasn't her fault, and I was used to it. It would be okay. I remember Julio coming and hugging me good-bye. He told me quietly that I needed to get on the weights and build up some strength and then deck Donnie when he talked to me that way. I knew he no longer had Donnie on that pedestal. Lexi was also very upset as we got in the pickup for our drive home. I couldn't stop crying, the humiliation of what just happened and being stuck in the car for two days with Donnie was more than I could handle.

About thirty minutes later, Donnie called his mom and apologized. Then he apologized to Lexi for behaving that way in front of her. He looked at me and asked if he had gone too far, overreacted. I just stared out the window and continued crying. I never got an apology, and it didn't matter.

I remember this moment as being very significant. I vowed to myself that this was going to be the last time Donnie made me cry. I would start to fight back, I would fight for Lexi. He would never get her from me. Right then, I remembered making my heart hard. I would feel nothing from here on out. No more pain, no more panic, no more anger. I would focus on getting out and making sure he did not get Lexi from me. My heart became like stone. From here on out when Donnie would throw his ideas out at me, or beg me to help him minister to hurting people, or tell me heartbreaking stories of other people's hardships, I would feel nothing. My heart became frozen solid. And around that rock-hard heart, I put a very tall stone wall. Nothing was going in and nothing was going out. And it worked for a while.

CHAPTER 13

Storm

Donnie returned to his job the day after we got home. I felt a break from him was well deserved. We were not getting along by any means. He was not happy that he would now be alone since Julio hadn't come with him. He kept saying things like, "God didn't intend for me to be alone, I'm not a lone ranger, I need to be around people." I was way beyond feeling sorry for Donnie. He began to pressure me to spend more time there with Lexi. I was struggling to keep things going at home, and quite honestly, Lexi was sick of going. There was nothing to do there while Donnie was working.

She was missing her sisters and her friends. She kept telling me it was not the way she wanted to spend her summer.

Donnie got a call from a lineman company that chases storms. Donnie was set on going. He would be going to New Jersey. His work agreed to let him go and then take him back. They were desperate for help. I wasn't sure Donnie could handle the pressure and sleeplessness of being on storm. Who was I kidding, he wasn't sleeping anyway.

Donnie kept telling me he knew he wasn't supposed to go alone. He asked Tommy to drop his job and go and also another lineman friend. He was very frustrated that neither of them would do it. Nobody in their right mind would consider leaving their full-time job to go on storm for a week or a month and then come back to no job. Yes, you make lots of money on storm, but that doesn't replace a full-time job. Donnie couldn't understand it, but then again, he didn't really want to work and seemed to enjoy being out of work. Donnie found Kevin, a high school student, to go with him on this storm.

Kevin was scheduled to go on a mission trip. He decided to go make big bucks with Donnie instead. He had no training, and again, Donnie had gotten him on and said he would teach him all he needed to know before they arrived.

It was a miracle in itself that Donnie got packed and got to the airport on time. Kevin and I had to do all the travel arrangements because Donnie kept getting frustrated and couldn't focus. Again, I was thrilled to see him go and we needed the money. When I questioned him as to why he was taking Kevin, he told me that God told him not to go alone. He told me that taking Kevin, a young Christian, would help keep Donnie accountable.

They left and I hoped I could relax a little. Every time Donnie goes on storm, whether he's manic or not, things go wrong at the house. This instance was no different. I had mower problems, shower problems, and I still had a huge mound in my yard from replacing the sewer last year. When we returned from vacation, I had knee-high corn growing solid on that mound. Donnie had thrown bird seed on it when I asked him to flatten out the mound.

I remember one day being excited to mow. Mowing was relaxing for me and I enjoyed it. I had just had my mower worked on, and shortly after I started mowing, it died. I had to push it uphill from the backyard to the front. This seemed to be a breaking point for me. I was in tears by the time I was done and I remember saying, "God must hate me." All I wanted to do was keep things up, keep things looking nice. Donnie had lost all interest in this and it was all up to me. I took pride in the way things looked. Couldn't I just mow my yard? Why did everything have to be so hard? And why was God making me go through all of this again with Donnie?

That is when the hives began. Panic attacks intensified and became more regular. I got sores on my scalp that popped up when I was stressed; all the same things that happened to me four years ago. I was angry. I was angry at Donnie and started to feel hatred toward him. And I was angry at God. So much for a rock-hard heart that was supposed to help me feel nothing.

I heard from Donnie often while he was gone, about every two or three hours. He was driving me crazy. I just wanted a break. The storm didn't happen, but I didn't care. They still got paid, and it kept Donnie away for at least a week.

I noticed a lot of changes while Donnie was gone. My best guess was that he was really trying to impress Kevin. And he did. When Donnie would call me, he would always be talking right in front of Kevin, and he would be praising me, how wonderful I was, how much he loved me. It was sickening and I was embarrassed how he was going on in front of a young high school kid. I asked him to stop, and if he felt he had to say all those things, then call me in private. Donnie called back about a minute later and said he would not apologize for loving his wife and he was trying to teach Kevin how to treat a wife. Are you serious? I wanted to puke.

Next thing you know, Donnie had handed the phone to his young passenger and he was telling me how awesome Donnie was and how he had never seen anybody so in tune with God. Yes, Donnie had done just what he wanted. He had put himself on a pedestal through Kevin's eyes. Donnie was full of himself like never before and Kevin was his biggest fan.

With storm duty over, the guys were trying to figure out how to get home. This was causing Donnie much frustration. They had flown out. Kevin had decided to head to Georgia to finish out his mission trip. So Donnie rented a car and drove him there. Donnie had left the decision up to Kevin, but as soon as Kevin was delivered, Donnie became angry. I could hear it on the phone. It was kind of a "I did this for him and now he left me all alone." Donnie had grown to hate being alone.

This brought about hours of Taylor and me helping Donnie search on line for ways to get home. We checked rental cars, buses, trains, and planes. I was all for a rental car because that would keep him away longer. I dreaded his coming home. At first, Donnie thought he should drive the rental because it would give him opportunities to pick up hitchhikers and witness to people all the way home.

Donnie hadn't slept and this was causing much emotional distress on him. He finally decided to have us set up airline tickets. We arranged for him to drop his rental car in Atlanta and board a plane there. He would fly into Minneapolis. He agreed to this, and the minute we accepted it online, he changed his mind. It was too late to back out; it was all paid for and confirmed. He was furious.

He arrived in the Atlanta airport with his flight not leaving until the next morning. Donnie refused to get a hotel. He was terrified in the airport. It was very overwhelming for him. He said it was huge and there were so many people. I know now that bipolar brings about euphoric behavior. The sights and sounds were multiplied many times in Donnie's head, and it was becoming too much. I had no sympathy. Taylor

| *Lori White*

and I had spent hours on the phone dealing with him, trying to help him, trying to please him. He must have changed his mind twenty times. Every time we would find a deal, he would want us to check something else and then he would decide he wanted the first deal, and by then, the deal was gone. It was exhausting.

By morning, Donnie called me to thank Taylor. He had been furious, but his night in the airport had been a blessing from God he said. Donnie was sure Satan had wanted him to drive all by himself to get home. God had showed him in the airport otherwise. Donnie announced that he was now a sports psychologist. He had met a basketball player and, of course, struck up a conversation with him. He had asked for Donnie's number because Donnie was so motivational. According to Donnie, this guy was going to call him so Donnie could get in his head and psych him up for games. Later, I would hear Donnie tell people he had become a sports psychologist. The guy never called.

Donnie also met a future wife for one of his friends who's divorced. The lady he sat by on the plane had quite a sad story, and of course, this drew Donnie in and he felt responsible to help. He asked her for her number so he could pass it along to his friend. Nothing came of this either.

I had to drive to Minneapolis to get Donnie from the airport. He was kind and grateful. The ride home wasn't bad; he was exhausted and slept some. Two things stuck out to me about the drive. One was Donnie telling me he knew God was telling him something big. I just kept nodding. I had no intentions of agitating him on his first day home. Donnie finally said, "I think I know what God is telling me." He then told me that God was telling him that he was supposed to run for president. I remember just praying that Donnie would keep this to himself. I also remember trying out my new coping mechanism. Nod, have a blank look on my face, block it out. Nod, nod, feel nothing. He asked me what I thought of him being president. I said, "Of the United States?" He told me yes. I said, "Are you sure God isn't just telling you to run for mayor or something before becoming president?" He was confident God was telling him he would be president of the United States. I went back to nodding and saying nothing.

The second thing that I remember about the ride was Donnie napping. He was exhausted, and he would fall asleep sitting straight up. All of a sudden, he would startle awake and act like he had a steering wheel in his hands. I could see on his face that he thought he had fallen asleep at the wheel. This happened several times, and once or twice, he actually grabbed the steering wheel from the passenger seat, almost causing us to wreck. I assumed this came from his hours of driving with no sleep. I was guessing from his behaviors that he had fallen asleep at the wheel many times.

Donnie also told me that he had started a tattoo of my name to show his love for me. I was not happy about this. I'm not a fan of tattoos, and for all I knew, we weren't going to stay married. I didn't want my name on his arm. When I told him we really couldn't afford to get tattoos, he assured me that he hadn't paid a dime for it. Donnie had taken up smoking, and right in front of Kevin, he had branded himself. He had four or five cigarette burns on his arm, the start of my name. He planned to finish it later. It looked raw and infected.

No one was impressed, especially me or my girls. In fact, Taylor told her dad it was stupid and he was outraged at her "lack of respect." It was embarrassing, and later, when other people started to question him and make fun of him, he changed his story. He told people he was in a tough man contest and the challenge had been the cigarette burns. Of course, in his story, he had not backed down.

CHAPTER 14

Help

The downward spiral of my life became worse. Donnie became more manic. Even though he was working an hour and a half away and I only saw him a few days every week, he continued to cause much stress to me. The story of his childhood that he insisted on telling everyone was becoming more and more depressing. Every time he told it, it sounded worse. I'm not trying to say that what Donnie had felt all his life was not real. He had every reason for heartache.

Donnie would tell of waiting at his mom's outside for hours, only to be forgotten. His dad was supposed to pick him up for a family dinner, and it wasn't until all the cousins were seated around the table that his dad realized he had forgotten him. He also was telling often how his dad used to take his stepchildren on fun vacations, and then when they returned, they would have Donnie and his sister out to hear how much fun they had and look at the pictures. I knew these stories were true as Donnie had shared them with me before his mania. These would be hurtful things to anybody, but to someone experiencing euphoric behavior, it was leaving a hole in his heart that seemed impossible to repair. Each time he told the stories, they sounded worse. He had had these hurts all his life, but now they were magnified to unbearable.

At this point, my coping mechanisms were wearing thin. I could still make my heart hard as stone and I would let myself feel nothing. But then when I did break down, it was like floodgates had opened. My chest felt tight all the time and my heart was staying hard, especially toward a God who didn't seem interested in rescuing me from this nightmare.

Denny and Erma checked on me often, either by stopping by or calling. Denny kept in contact with Donnie and they agreed he needed help. But since he wouldn't get help, Erma convinced me that I had to get myself some help. I had to stay strong for my girls. She suggested a Christian organization called The Living Center. It was a place I could go for counseling. She asked me if she could set up an appointment for me.

I wish I had kept a journal four years ago and also when things started to repeat themselves but I didn't. Some things run together and sometimes events are hard to keep in order. I'm not sure, but I think at this time, Donnie was spending more time at home trying to "start" his own business.

He had some cash in his pocket from the storm. He planned to start his own handy man business. He had also applied a couple of places for maintenance work. He had made several contacts for another business opportunity. This latest one would take approximately $75,000 to start up. Donnie searched high and low for someone to invest and fund his new adventure. Anyone who visited with Donnie for two minutes knew that something wasn't right. He actually made contact with a few people who had the money to help him. He was infuriated that people wouldn't just hand over that kind of money to him. When he would share his frustrations, I would stare at him, blank, feeling nothing

He started to line up jobs for his handyman business. He planned to employ Toby and another young man he was helping. He also thought he could help out the guy's dad who was disabled. Toby worked on the farm for his dad and wasn't usually available. The other man suffered from depression and I suspected drug use. He wasn't reliable at all. The dad was very reliable; he just couldn't do physical labor. Donnie always paid him more because he could organize jobs and give foreman directions; he was knowledgeable according to Donnie.

Donnie had no idea how to run a business. There was no pay scale, he had no idea how to bid jobs, and if people couldn't pay, he would do it for little to nothing and still pay his employees well. The first few jobs he did, he either barely broke even or went in the hole. The storm money was going fast.

Donnie continued to run his mouth all over town. Anyone he saw with small children was told to go have a date and we would watch their children. We had done this for people often and didn't mind, but he was going to the extreme. What he was really saying was drop them off and Lori will watch them because Donnie was never home. One day, I got a message from a girl I barely knew. She said Donnie had told her we would babysit her two children for free. She worked evenings and nights. She went on to give me her work schedule for the next two weeks and ask for our address. She planned to start this new babysitting service the next night. I had to contact her and tell her I was not doing babysitting for free or for pay. I told her I did not want to bring two small children with me to Kaylee's volleyball games. I asked Donnie to stop broadcasting this to people. He said he would make sure to make himself more clear next time.

Through all of this, I was losing it. I remember asking Tommy and Beth to just commit me. I was willing, if they would drive me, I couldn't do it anymore. All Beth had to do was remind me that my girls needed me. So when Erma suggested I get counseling, I agreed. Donnie thought this was great, he said I needed help.

Erma had offered to drive me to my out-of-town appointment, but I wanted to go alone. It took just under an hour to get there and that time of driving was like heaven for me; peace and quiet and a day away from my husband.

As I entered the building the first time, I sat and waited for my appointment time. I began to have a panic attack. The tears were hard to control. I tried to get it together before my appointment started.

When I was called in, I met with two ladies. It was explained to me that they always counsel in twos. One of the counselors asked me why I had come. I began to sob. I held up my hands. They were shaking uncontrollably. Through my tears and sobs, I told the ladies I couldn't do this anymore. I explained to them what had been happening.

The head counselor looked at me and explained to me how things worked there. They told me they were going to pray with me. I said no and told them I had prayed my guts out and I couldn't pray anymore, and I was pretty sure God wasn't listening. She looked at me and said, "This won't work if you don't pray with us." They told me they would guide me.

They did guide me. At first, everything was just questions that I answered. Slowly, they invited God into our conversation. The first visit brought me strength, and I agreed to come back the following week.

By my second visit, I was more relaxed. This counseling session had little to do with Donnie. That is what forced me there, but that was it. The sessions were about helping me cope with my life. When we would start to pray together, they would ask me what I saw. I saw purple and sometimes black nothing. That was it. Every time I closed my eyes and began to relax and pray, I would see purple. When the counselors would mention Donnie, the purple would disappear and I would see darkness. When they would redirect me to God, I would again see purple.

On my third visit, the counselor told me she had been looking over the notes and she felt the color purple was a sign of protection for me. She asked me what the first thing I thought of when I heard the word purple. I told her in our church there is a rugged cross, and at Easter, there is always a purple sash draped over it.

We began to pray. I will never forget this third visit. As they guided me in prayer through things that were now my everyday life, I began to get an image of Jesus. The women had me describe this to them. Everything they brought up produced an image for me. I would begin my journey of talking with Jesus, seeing purple. When they would mention Donnie, my heart would begin to race and I would feel panic. Then an image of Jesus would come to my mind. The picture was vivid. Jesus would stand in front of me, His arm extended. His hand would be over my heart holding me back. This was Jesus telling me not to go before him. As I would begin to relax, bright light would come out of his hand and into my heart. I would feel strength and be refreshed. Then everything would fade into purple.

This happened over and over through our counseling sessions. One of the counselors explained to me that she had been doing this for years, and she had never encountered anybody who had the mental pictures like I did. They explained that they felt this was a coping mechanism. They wanted me to go home and try something. When Donnie would stress me out and frustrate me, they wanted me to just walk away, breath deep, close my eyes and think of purple, and immediately start talking to Jesus.

I was eager to try this out. Just seeing Donnie when I pulled in the driveway was enough to let me try right away. It worked. As soon as I started to calm my breathing and pray, the purple appeared. Shortly after, I was able to picture myself behind Jesus. He was protecting me and He would not let me go before him, He would not let me go alone.

I cannot tell you how much relief this brought me. I was able to control my actions better and not let my fear and anger get the best of me. The panic attacks became fewer and I felt God was back in control.

I remember praying on the way home, and out loud, I said, "God, where have you been?" My reply was, "I have been right here. The question is where have *you* been?" What I know now is that God was in control the whole time when I let Him. The counselors at The Living Center helped me get my focus back on God. After a month, I didn't feel I needed to go any more. Were things better with Donnie? No, they were worsening by the day. But my focus was on God. God got me through this four years ago, and He would get me through it again. I had to be strong for my girls.

I went back to The Living Center one more time. I wanted to thank them for helping me get my focus back on God. I wanted to tell them I was doing okay. On the day of the appointment, I almost didn't go, but God was really prompting me to. I went and I was so glad I did. The ladies thanked me and told me that most people just stop coming and leave them wondering how things were going. I provided some closure for them and they told me to keep them updated and come back if I needed to. They asked me about Donnie. I told them we had a psychiatric appointment and that it had been scheduled for several months and was still a few weeks away.

Right then, I knew why God had prompted me to go. The counselor gave me the name of a Christian psychologist. I knew Donnie would be more apt to keep an appointment if he knew the person was a Christian. I called as soon as I got in my car. Yes, they could see Donnie. They could see him tomorrow. Unreal. All the months we had to wait on an appointment and now I could get in tomorrow. I told them I needed more time. Like I said, events are mixed up and at this time Donnie was working some and couldn't get off that quick. The doctor would be on vacation then so we would have to wait. The appointment ended up being one week later than the psychiatrist appointment, but I didn't really plan on Donnie keeping that appointment anyway. And we had waited three months, so what was one more week.

When I got home, I told Donnie I had changed his appointment. I explained to him that he would be seeing a Christian psychologist. He was very excited by this news and said he couldn't wait. Neither could I. I was finally going to have a diagnosis for Donnie.

CHAPTER 15

The Psychologist

Donnie was blaming most of our marriage problems on me putting the kids first our whole married life. So he suggested we go to his psychologist appointment together and make a weekend of it. I agreed, I was afraid not to, afraid he would back out of the appointment.

The psychologist was great. He listened. Donnie talked for what seemed like forever. Every detail about his miserable childhood, he told how I had always put the girls first, he told about what happened four years ago, and what he believed was happening now.

When it was my turn, I pretty much said what I had said in the ER that day. Donnie had an episode of manic behavior four years ago, then depression. Now it is starting over. He has racing thoughts and can't follow through or complete a task.

The psychologist was so kind when he told Donnie that he had the symptoms of bipolar disorder. I was filled with joy. Maybe now, Donnie would see he needed medication. The doctor did go on to explain that medication can control a lot of the bipolar behavior.

That was it. Donnie said maybe he would come back and see him for counseling about his childhood issues. We headed to the casino as we would be staying in the hotel there for the night. As we were walking around outside, Donnie called his dad and then his mom. I could not believe my ears. Donnie was telling about his appointment and he was telling them that the doctor said he did *not* have bipolar. The things he was saying and explaining were not even said at the appointment. Yet I could see that Donnie had heard them. He wasn't just trying to pull something over on them, he really believed what he was saying. Yet part of him knew, I think, because he kept reassuring both of his parents that I was standing right there. I think he thought he sounded more believable if they thought he was talking right in front of me.

That night at bedtime, Donnie got ready to leave me alone in the room and go gamble. He asked me to come with him and I said no. So he decided to go by himself. Once he left the room, I left the room. I went for a walk outside in the dark. While out, I texted family and friends who were waiting to hear how the appointment had gone. I told them all that he had been diagnosed but did not believe it. I stayed away for a long time until I saw Donnie walking around outside. I let him wonder for a while where I was. He talked to every person that walked past. Finally, I came back. Donnie asked me where I had been and I told him I had been out. That was it. He didn't ask any questions.

I asked him how the blackjack table had treated him that night. He had always lit up at this question lately but not tonight. He said he hadn't done well. Then he told me it was because I wasn't in there with him, supporting him.

CHAPTER 16

Out of Control

D onnie returned to his job an hour and a half away. I was on edge at all times, even when he was gone. The best thing I could have done was return to The Living Center, but I didn't. Daily, I would turn things over to God and tell Him I couldn't do it anymore. Daily, I would take it back and try to control my crazy life.

All of us were on edge. Donnie talked more and more about starting his own business as this would help every unemployed person in our town. He had stepped aside from the handyman work he was doing but kept lining up jobs and promising people work. In fact, several people would knock on my door and call our house, wondering when Donnie was going to be able to employ them. Several people were ready to walk away from a steady job to work for Donnie. The promises I was being told he had made were enough to make me sick. I begged him to stop running his mouth. I told him young men were ready to quit jobs to work for him with a company that didn't exist. This enraged him. He could see how they were excited to work for him, but he was adamant he had not made these promises. Really? How could five or six people be knocking on my door and calling with the same story?

Donnie became obsessed with music, loud music. In the car, in the house, in the garage, outside, anywhere he was, music had to be blaring. He started to listen to songs from his younger years. He said these songs had a Christian meaning behind them. I didn't buy it, not when there was so much profanity in them. You know the music is too loud when the teenagers in the house are asking for it to be turned down. One time, while we were eating supper, Kaylee asked if we could turn down the music. This infuriated Donnie; he stomped across the room, turned the music off, and took his food to the garage.

Donnie seemed to be stuck at age fifteen. The music, the way he was dressing, the way he was obsessed with himself, his body. He ran around half dressed most of the time, flaunting his finely toned muscles. Little things like changing from briefs to boxers. This wouldn't be a big deal except for the fact that he liked his boxers hanging out of the top of his pants. Starting to smoke at age forty-three? Who does this? His energy level was definitely that of a teenager as well as his feeling of being invincible. Tommy had also made the comment that Donnie seemed to be stuck in a teenager frame of mind.

Everywhere Donnie went, he had to carry a briefcase. I think it made him feel professional and important. Everything was in that case: receipts, contact information, business cards, newspapers, magazines. He was always losing things and forever searching that stupid briefcase. No matter how important he looked, I'm sure the ladies at the local truck stop weren't impressed. One day, I got a call from them telling me Donnie had driven off without paying for his gas. I knew his mind was cluttered and it had been an accident, but it was humiliating just the same. I had to drive out and pay for the gas. I told Donnie later and he laughed. He said he was lucky he knew the ladies working or they probably would have called the police.

Donnie preached nonstop. I don't mean just a tidbit here and there, I mean full-blown sermons. He preached mostly to me because I was the one with all the problems, according to him. I felt I was going crazy. Anything I confronted him with, he threw a verse at me. I had enough sanity left to be able to recognize the fact that he was twisting the scriptures to fit his bad behavior. Yet even though I knew this, I felt like I was fighting Donnie and God.

Taylor had asked her dad over and over to stop trying to fix everybody's problems in town and fix the ones at home.

She felt he was putting everyone first before his family. She was right. Taylor was car shopping that summer. She had bought her car and was ready to sell it and get something more dependable as she would be driving to classes starting in the fall. I remember someone coming to look at Taylor's car that was for sale. This was not a department I felt comfortable in helping Taylor with and she was not comfortable doing it alone. She asked her dad for help. I remember Taylor coming in the house close to tears. Donnie agreed to help her. He told the people looking at her car that if they thought this one was too high, he had a friend who was selling a great car at a great price, and he would be happy to take them to look at that car. This was a prime example of how Donnie was putting everyone's needs before his families. Taylor wasn't asking too much for her car and she hoped to get as much out of it as she could. Donnie seemed to be trying to talk the people out of buying it from the beginning.

Taylor was really a rock for me. She kept me level headed. When I did blow up, she would tell me how stupid it was and the damage it had caused by angering her dad. She gave me constant advice and how to react to all of Donnie's idiosyncrasies. I counted on her a lot during this time.

Four years ago, Kaylee had sided with her dad. She had been in denial up to this point that what happened four years ago was happening again. I could tell that she was starting to believe it. Donnie had gone to the pool several times and embarrassed Kaylee while she was working. He had badmouthed a classmate of hers to another classmate. This took about two minutes to circulate back to that person. He was hanging out at the weight room and school with all of her friends. Kaylee was becoming frustrated.

Lexi was suffering greatly. Four years ago, she was young enough that I could protect her from everything. Not now. She asked a lot of questions about her dad's behavior. She knew it wasn't right and it scared her. For example, her dad had a talk with her one day. She had heard a filthy term. She wanted to know what it was. Donnie explained and told her it was not a naughty word but an actual thing and people had chosen to make it naughty. He gave her permission to say it whenever she wanted. He also explained that other words that were considered swear words were also real words that people had made naughty. He gave her permission to say swear words when she wanted, as long as she was using them correctly. I had a long talk with Lexi about this, and she knew already that these words were not to come out of her mouth.

I continued to rejoice when Donnie was gone. When he was home from work, we hardly saw him. He was pushing me a lot to "minister" to Toby and his girlfriend. I wanted no part of this. I could barely breathe when he was around, and I knew he had no business helping or giving anyone advice.

One day in the middle of the week, I got a call from Donnie. He told me he had asked for a transfer at work. He would be moving four hours away from us. I asked him why he would do this. None of it made sense. He was constantly complaining about working away from home and was going to be moving from an hour and a half away to four hours away by choice. He told me that he wanted to be closer to his brother. He said that they were planning to start up a new business together so he needed to be close so they could plan. I reminded him that right now, I brought Lexi to see him every week for several days. I told him I would not do this if he was four hours away. I asked him if he understood what I was saying. He said he did.

I don't really remember what happened at this point. Things weren't good when Donnie left. The farther away from home he got, the worse things got. By the time he left, we were barely speaking and our marriage was holding on by a thread. I had no doubt that we would not reach our twenty-fifth wedding anniversary in August.

One thing I know we were fighting about was a paycheck from his storm duty. He put part of his pay in our checking account. But a check that came later he was carrying around in his pocket. Before he left, I asked him for the check. Donnie was using four credit cards and two of them were close to maxed out. At this point, I was paying close to $600 a month on credit card payments and our income was far from steady. I explained this and he became enraged. He told me that he was going to use that check for his new company and I wasn't touching it. He took the check with him when he left.

I felt pure hatred for him after that. I would question God how it was possible to love someone yet hate them with your every being. Once in a while, God would tug on my heart. The day that Donnie was to start his new job, God was prodding me to contact him and check in on him. I didn't want to talk to him, and God and I argued about this for quite a while. Finally, I decided to text him. Donnie and I had been talking divorce a lot, and this new voluntary move was not helping matters. I text him and told him that I hoped he was having a good day and that his job was going well.

This was a huge mistake. Within minutes, Donnie called me very angry. How dare I text and confuse him, acting like I care. He wanted a divorce. He would call me many more times in the following hour, crying every time. By the end of the day, he was no longer employed. I asked if he was fired. He said he told them he was having marriage problems and needed some time off. Unemployed. I assumed he was fired for sitting talking on the phone all day, and I felt confident they noticed he couldn't complete a task. I was convinced Donnie didn't want to work anyway.

Donnie asked me to come to him. I told him no. I reminded him that he went there by choice and that I had told him I was not going to be coming four hours every week to see him. He told me if I didn't come, then he wanted a divorce. Donnie left the town he had just gotten to and told me he was heading to our hometown to stay at his mom's for a while. If someone would have told me that things were about to get worse, I would have argued that things couldn't get any worse. I was wrong. All hell was about to break loose.

CHAPTER 17

Hometown

Donnie went to stay at his mom's. I didn't hear from her much and this frustrated me. I knew she knew what was going on. I hoped and prayed Donnie would crash soon, he had the signs of doing so according to his first episode. Every time I thought the crash was coming, he would pull out of it. I was hoping it would happen while he was in our hometown and then his mom could care for him while he laid in the bed wallowing in his sorrow. I was beyond sympathetic.

Our hometown is five hours away from where we live. I guess that isn't far enough. Donnie continued to wreak havoc on our lives even from that distance. Donnie's sister Tammy had been in constant contact with me. At times, I felt she was one of the few of Donnie's family members who believed me. I knew I could trust her, and she became my sister like never before. I could not have made it through this horrible time without her.

Tammy and I talked daily. Tammy lives in our hometown, and so when Donnie started running his mouth and running around all night long, she was notified. Donnie was spending a lot of time at the casino and other bars in town. People were talking to Donnie's mom and his sister, asking what was wrong with him. People were coming into my mom's place of employment telling her that Donnie needed help.

A lot of things happened during this time and I managed to hear about all of them. Donnie was telling the whole town that we were getting a divorce. He had taken his check and opened an account in our hometown. When I questioned him, he told me it was because we were going to move there and it would be there waiting for us.

Donnie spent every night at the bars and casino. I started to notice cash advances on the credit card bills and also money being taken from our checking and savings account. All of these withdrawals were done at the casino. We had no income and I was struggling to pay the bills. Donnie was winning big apparently. People had seen him at the casino giving away his winnings. I am talking over a thousand dollars being given away while I was trying to figure out how to pay the bills.

Donnie had told people that he had fallen asleep on his way there. He wasn't sleeping at all except for a power nap here and there. He was on a two-lane highway with his pickup and trailer. Next thing he knew, he had crossed lanes and woke up driving in the opposite ditch. His nephew had questioned him when he saw his truck grill full of grass. Months later, when Donnie would recount this story to me, he told me I might as well have been a widow at that time. He could have been killed or killed someone else.

At one point, a relative called me and asked me if Donnie was using drugs. I said absolutely not. Apparently, Donnie had bragged to a family member that he had smoked pot with our neighbors down the street.

That was it. I was done. I could not do this anymore. I questioned Donnie about the pot. He told me it was true. He said he had only done it once and it was no big deal. He claimed it was all natural, merely a weed, so no harm done. He was furious at the person he had told for sharing the information. Donnie's sister told me that she did not want to see him. She refused to go to her mom's where Donnie was staying.

Donnie's mom, like everybody else, didn't know what to do and she didn't want to be around him any more than I did. Once Donnie borrowed their motorcycle; I'm not sure why they let him borrow it other than she might have been scared of him, like I was. Donnie wasn't afraid to drive after drinking. He said he was never drunk and it wasn't a problem. Anyway, Donnie had been out all night, and when he finally headed home with no sleep, he decided to wash the motorcycle before returning it. Turns out he washed the keys down the drain at the car wash. His mom was upset about this.

From there, Donnie decided to go to the local motorcycle shop to ask about getting a key made. While there, he talked them into "lending" him a motorcycle. He gave his stepdad's name and the owner knew him and decided it was probably okay. I'm not sure how this all played out, but the owner called Donnie's mom before letting Donnie take the motorcycle. His lack of sleep and manic behavior had caused the owner to suspect drug use. His mom told the guy it wasn't drugs but to not lend him a motorcycle.

The stories went on and on. Donnie soon grew bored in our hometown and went back to the area his brother lived in. He had big business plans to figure out. This gave me an opportunity. With a little help, I started to make a plan.

CHAPTER 18

The Plan

I was desperate. I had contacted a lawyer about how to keep Donnie away from Lexi. I was told I couldn't unless he harmed her. Once I found out about all the things in Osceola, I knew I had to start using my head and stop letting him walk on me.

First, I went to our bank to make sure he couldn't get into our girls' savings accounts. I had access to them through my online banking. Some double checking showed that he did not. I also found out there was no way of keeping him from taking money from our accounts. So I began to take money from our accounts. I had a hiding place that only Taylor knew about, in case something happened to me. I will tell you at this point I was very afraid of Donnie and I didn't feel safe even when he was four or five hours away. I constantly looked over my shoulder and I was very jumpy.

Next, a friend went to the local sheriff department. They told them what was going on and asked about protecting Lexi. Again, I could get no help. I could not keep him away from her. They advised me to have her in my sight at all times. He could not take her from me, but if he took her when she wasn't with me, I would have the same stipulations getting her back. The only way I could get a restraining order was if he physically hurt me or one of the girls. According to the law, he could take Lexi; she was half his.

I was frantic. I watched my back at all times. When I would go to the store, I would find a place for Lexi, then I would scan the parking lot and watch over my shoulder the whole time. This is a terrifying way to live and I was exhausted. My hands never stopped shaking. I couldn't eat. I had trouble sleeping.

I heard from Donnie occasionally now. That was way too often. I didn't want to hear from him at all. At times, I begged God to just take him, let him fall asleep driving, and instantly be in Jesus's arms. Then this would all be over for all of us, including him. These thoughts occurred often and now they shame me.

Desperate times call for desperate measures. In one of Donnie's phone conversations, he told me he was having supper at his brother's. Tammy had talked to her brother and said that if other family members met there, then maybe everybody together could convince Donnie to check himself in. In the few times I had talked to him, I felt he was very vulnerable due to lack of sleep. Tammy told me to call her brother; he wanted to talk to me. I called him. On the phone, he sounded like he was on board. He would get Donnie fed and give him a few beers, then everybody could show up. He told me that it would take three people to have him committed. This was news to me and I had done my research. But I believed him. Later, I would find out that he was telling me one thing and telling his sister he didn't quite believe me. He thought Donnie and I were having marriage problems and that I was trying to keep Lexi from him. I don't believe he had any intentions of helping me.

The other hitch was that Tammy felt it would benefit to have her dad there. I told her I wasn't going to be there and she was, so whatever she thought. She called her dad. Then, he called me. He asked me what was going on. I could tell he wasn't on board. Within minutes after hanging up, Donnie called me. He was furious. He said his dad had called him and said I was making a plan to have him committed. I played dumb. Donnie told me he was taking off and no one would find him. He told me to contact a lawyer and that he wanted half custody of Lexi.

I began to bawl and scream. I remember Tommy and Beth being here with me while we were all trying to set the plan in motion. I text Donnie's dad and said thanks a lot. He tried to call me shortly after and I didn't answer. I called Tammy to tell her what had happened. The plan was ruined. We had been so close and now Donnie was enraged, enraged like I have never seen him before.

Donnie had been right about one thing. We couldn't find him. I searched the area for casinos. I called around. No one would give me information. He was hiding. The next morning, I would find him when I checked my online banking and saw that we had one hundred dollars left in our savings account. The withdrawal had come from a casino.

CHAPTER 19

The Meeting

D onnie stayed away for a while. His mom promised to stall him and let me know if she found out he was headed for home. He would call the home phone and ask for Lexi. He made no conversation with me.

Tammy let me know that an uncle had died. This was a man that had been married to Donnie's aunt several years ago. Donnie remembered Pete taking him fishing, something he had always dreamed of having his dad do. According to Donnie, Pete had treated Donnie better than his dad ever had. Lately, all of Donnie's rage seemed to be pointed at me and his dad.

Tammy said Donnie was taking the death hard. He was going to head to our hometown to attend the funeral. Tammy didn't think any other family members were going, no one was that close to him and hadn't seen him for years as he and their aunt had divorced. Tammy wasn't sure why Donnie was taking it so hard. It was very sad as any death is, but according to Tammy, Donnie wasn't that close to him. It was reminding me of four years ago when Donnie's cousin had passed away. A sad event like that is magnified greatly when you are having euphoric behavior.

On his way to our hometown, Donnie called me. I hadn't heard from him in a while. I asked what he had been doing, if he was working. This angered him. He explained he worked all day, going around, lining up jobs, getting contacts, helping people who needed help. Then he told me about his Uncle Pete. I could tell he was devastated. He asked me to go to the funeral with him. I told him no. I barely remembered Pete and I had no desire to be anywhere near Donnie. He told me if I didn't go, then he wanted a divorce. I told him to go ahead and file. I wasn't doing it. If he wanted a divorce, he could pay for it and also for the custody battle.

He said he wanted to see Lexi. He asked me to meet him halfway so he could see her. This got to my heart. He sounded vulnerable and I knew how much he loved his kids. Lexi was also missing her dad, even though she was scared to be around him. I told him I would come if I could get someone else to be there. I told him I didn't feel safe without someone else there. I was very surprised this didn't anger him and he accepted this condition without argument.

Donnie told me he was going to invite his dad along. I don't know if he ever called him or not. Donnie later told me his dad wasn't coming. I told him I would call my brother to see if he was free. I knew I was asking a lot. My brother farms and any spare time he has is spent at his kids' sporting events. And it was fair time and the kids showed pigs. I hated to ask but didn't feel I had much choice. I was afraid to not take Lexi. I knew it would enrage Donnie and I was afraid he would try to take her if I didn't go along with the visit.

My brother agreed to go. Donnie wanted to meet at a lake. He wanted to swim with Lexi. I got there first, then my brother. I knew Donnie would be late. I figured he would be sidetracked many times. I was right.

While we were waiting, my brother, Greg, asked me if we had a canoe. I said no. He said, "You do now." I looked in the direction he was looking and here comes Donnie with a canoe-shaped object strapped to the top of his pickup.

We did our greeting and I asked about the wrapped item on top of the truck. He said it was surprise for our family and it had been free. It was a brand-new canoe. I asked who had given him a brand-new canoe. He said he had bought it. I told him that if he bought it, then it wasn't free. He considered it free because he had bought it with casino winnings. I refrained from commenting.

Donnie and Lexi went out in the canoe. They went around the lake. We could see them at all times. I saw Donnie get out and pick up a huge rock. Donnie knows I love rocks. When we vacation, I always bring home beautiful rocks as souvenirs. He put the rock in the canoe. When they returned to the beach, Donnie asked me to talk with him by the truck. My brother stayed with Lexi while she swam and I followed Donnie, lugging the large rock on his shoulder. I was trembling with fear.

Once we were at the truck, Donnie opened the back and took out a large, Rubbermaid container. It was full of stuff from a Goodwill store. There was a torn Dolphin jersey, a few knickknacks for me, and some plastic mugs. Then he took out a picture frame with a paper in it that someone had printed off their computer. It was a scripture verse, 2 Corinthians 5:17. It said, "Therefore, if anyone is in Christ, he is a new creation; the old has gone, the new has come." Donnie pointed to it with tears in his eyes and said, "This is what has happened to me." He went on to tell me he wanted to go into ministry; he went over the whole story of wanting to help people, starting the business, etc. Then he said, "You are either with me or against me." I didn't comment.

Then he told me that he wanted me to move around with him. He asked me if I remembered the old TV show, *The Promised Land*. I did. This was about a family who traveled around in a camper helping people. He told me God was telling him that Lexi and I were supposed to travel with him.

If he went on storm for three weeks, Lexi and I were to go along. If he transferred to a new job, Lexi and I would move with him. I asked him about school. He told me I had my teaching degree and I could homeschool Lexi. I told him the demands he was making were too much and that I would not agree to it.

That was it. He was calm in a scary way. His eyes were wild; I swear I could see the devil in his eyes. A chill ran up my back. He told me he wanted a divorce and that he would give me money for bills. He told me the only thing he wanted was split custody of Lexi. He told me he would never walk out on her the way his dad walked out on him. I freaked out. I told him he would never get custody of Lexi; he wasn't stable and I would let everybody know he was a looney tune. Those were the words I used. I frantically walked to my brother and told him Lexi and I were leaving. I filled him in on what had just been demanded of me. I asked him to help Donnie put the canoe back on the truck.

I got Lexi out of the lake. She looked scared when she saw me. I told her we were leaving. My brother walked with me to the truck and Donnie came to tell Lexi good-bye. He hugged Lexi and whispered something in her ear. We left.

Greg let me know he had helped Donnie with the canoe and Donnie had been calm. Greg had told Donnie nobody could meet the demands he had laid out. Donnie wouldn't budge, he said it was my choice and he wanted a divorce. Greg said there was no getting through to him.

Lexi was terrified as we left. I asked her what her dad had said in her ear. Donnie had told Lexi he was going to come for her. She kept asking me what this meant. I told her I didn't know. I told her I would protect her. She told me she didn't want to spend time with her daddy, that he was scaring her. She kept looking out the back window of the vehicle to see if he was behind us.

We pulled over. I told her Donnie had headed back to our hometown, in the other direction. She asked if she could call her dad to ask what he had meant when he said he would be coming for her. I let her call. She asked and Donnie told her he just meant that he would be coming to see her soon. He would be coming after the funeral of his uncle. This seemed to put Lexi at some ease.

We stopped many times on the way home. In a weak moment, Donnie had the bank in our hometown send me paperwork to get my name on the account. I had sent it in and had a debit card in my purse. I never found an ATM that would let me take more than one or two hundred out at a time, so we stopped at every town and withdrew money. I stopped after $600 because I didn't want to anger Donnie. At each visit, I also took money out of our own checking account. I knew if I didn't, it would be gone soon. Again, I didn't take too much as I didn't want to anger Donnie. By the time I got home, I had $1,200 cash in my hand.

When we got home, Tammy assured me Donnie was at his mom's, so again, he was five hours away. Lexi and I were physically and emotionally drained. Lexi asked to sleep in my bed and she did this for several nights after. Each night, she would ask to lock the bedroom door. My precious girl was terrified that her dad was going to come and take her. I knew I had to take matters into my own hands. I had asked for help everywhere I could. There was no way to make him take meds, no way to get him into counseling, no way to get him committed. I had had enough.

By the time I returned home, Tommy and Beth had notified the sheriff department in town. They told them that I was scared and that he had threatened to take Lexi. They promised to do several drivebys day and night and also to stop if they saw anything suspicious. Lexi never left my sight, not for a minute. I lined up a safe place for me and all three girls here in town if needed. A place I knew Donnie could not find us. I lined up two more safe places for Lexi, one in town and one out of town. If I felt threatened, I would break every law and hide Lexi from her dad. He was not going to endanger her with his sleepless manic behavior.

CHAPTER 20

Plan B

It is hard to write each day, reliving what has happened. I usually write for an hour, not being able to take more. When I'm done with that hour, my body is tense, and usually, I have hives. Part 1 was easier to write. I could still remember most of it, but not the tiny details. Part 1 is far enough in the past that it isn't so horrifying any more.

Part 2 has been hard. It is very fresh, every detail still stuck in my brain. I am leaving out so many minor details and trying to only include the significant ones. I knew as I got farther into part 2 that there would be some hard chapters to write. This is one of those chapters.

I was scared. I feared Donnie would take Lexi. I was scared that Donnie would physically hurt me. I was scared he would kill somebody driving without sleep. I felt like I was living in a horror film.

I had some cash stashed, safe places lined up, plans formulated for emergencies, yet still I lived in fear. A friend told me that at one point, she had gotten a temporary separation from her husband. This kept him away from her and it also kept him from being able to see his child. I decided this was my next step. I would do whatever it took to keep Lexi safe. I didn't think Donnie would ever hurt Lexi on purpose. I just knew his judgment was off, and I did fear he would take her and hide.

I made an appointment with the same attorney my friend had used. I took Beth with me and also my friend Tasha. I was at the end of my rope. I couldn't stop crying and shaking. My heart was always beating hard and fast. I couldn't think clear. I was going through the motions of breathing and putting one foot in front of the other. I needed help. I was desperate.

By the time I got to the attorney, I couldn't control my crying. Beth and Tasha had to do all the talking. The attorney told me that there was a way to have Donnie committed. He explained that if he was putting others in danger, it could be done. I told him I was scared of him, yet in my heart, I knew he would never hurt me on purpose. The attorney told me that his driving without sleep would be enough to have him committed; he could kill somebody else if he fell asleep. The plan was put in motion. I was relieved but continued to cry.

At the time, I wasn't sure where Donnie was, but I assumed he would be in our hometown again after the funeral. He had a place to stay there, food, and a casino. The attorney told me I needed two people who knew what was going on. I called and asked my brother and Donnie's sister Tammy for help. They were both more than willing to help me. Tammy was terrified Donnie would kill himself or take Lexi and put her in danger. She did make me promise that I would not keep Lexi from her daddy. I told her I never would. That wouldn't be fair to Donnie or Lexi. I told her this was just until he was better and promised to get some kind of supervised visits lined up.

Greg and Tammy had to go to the courthouse in our hometown. They had to fill out a complaint. Tammy knew most of what had happened here at home, and she knew what he had been doing in our hometown as well. She had to write out everything. She included everything she knew: driving without sleep, gambling, drinking, smoking, pot use, on and on. Everyone knows that these things, minus the smoking pot, are not illegal. However, when you start them at age forty-three, when you are in a manic state of mind, I guess it was enough to accomplish what I thought was impossible.

It was done. I asked the attorney how it would work. The city police in our hometown were notified. They would be watching for him. And if he showed up at his mom's, they would be notified and come pick him up. They would cuff him and take him to a mental facility. I wanted to puke. I wanted to die. How could I do this to my husband? He couldn't help what he was doing; I knew that in my heart. He was ill. Beth and Tasha stayed with me and reassured me over and over that I was doing what was best for our family, protecting Lexi, and even doing what was best for Donnie. He needed help. I didn't know if I could ever forgive myself.

Few people knew about this. I did not tell Donnie's dad. I had learned my lesson. Donnie's mom knew, and though she cried, she knew it had to be done. She hoped she wouldn't be there when it happened. I hoped she wouldn't either. I told my mom and Greg, Tammy, Beth, and Tasha knew. That was it. I didn't tell my girls. The information wasn't ever leaked. Donnie made no contact with anyone. He was never picked up because he never came back to our hometown as we thought he would.

Donnie would let his sister know later that he went back to the area where his brother lived. The plan had failed again. That was my last hope. I had tried everything I could think of. There was nothing left to do but wait for the crash that would bring him out of his manic behavior and into depression. I prayed daily for this. Each time I prayed for it, I would ask God to forgive me. I remembered well four years ago. I felt like I had watched Donnie die a little each day, stuck in a hopeless depression. How could I pray for this to happen again? What kind of person would do this? A desperate person; that is the only answer I have.

One of the things that made this chapter close to impossible to write was that I have not yet had the courage to tell Donnie about my plan. He will hear about it for the first time when he reads my words. I am still sickened by it, can still picture it in my head, him being picked up and cuffed. I know Donnie will forgive me, but I still struggle to forgive myself.

CHAPTER 21

Eye-Opener

Donnie was gone for quite a while and we heard from him little. He would call Taylor and Kaylee to talk to Lexi. The few times I did talk to him, he asked me for a divorce. Every time, I told him if he wanted one, he could file. When I would say this, he would threaten me, telling me how sorry I would be if he filed. I think I was still holding out hope that my husband would come back to me. Also, I felt pretty confident that he was not focused enough to follow through on filing for a divorce.

With him absent for a while, I began to relax a little. I began to be able to function. I never stopped looking over my shoulder expecting to see him, and I remained prepared for emergencies, but I felt I could breathe a little easier.

With this, I began to be able to pray again. Just like I had done at The Living Center, I began to refocus on God. I remembered that God was in control. God was protecting me and the girls and even Donnie. The more I prayed and turned things over to God, the better I felt. I remember closing my eyes and seeing purple again. Then I would get that beautiful vision of Jesus protecting me.

I don't remember where I was when I fully listened to God. I don't remember what I was doing. But I do remember what God told me. It was like my eyes were opened. Yes, Donnie was sick and out of control, but some of what he was saying I couldn't deny. I had always put the girls first. That was easy to do when they are little and it became a habit. God showed me too, that if I knew Donnie was sick, then I needed to be more patient. God and I went a few rounds with this one. I felt I had been beyond patient. God told me He was in control. Then God told me that if Donnie was sick, and if he was that upset about his uncle dying, I should have been there when he asked me to come to the funeral.

It didn't matter that I hardly knew Pete. It didn't matter that Donnie was manic. My husband had needed me and begged me to come and I hadn't. I was wrong. I knew then that God was telling me to go to Donnie now. Now was the time that he would listen and that we could work things out and get help together.

I called Donnie. He didn't answer right away. When he did call me back, I told him I was going to come to where he was first thing in the morning. He told me not to come. He told me he didn't want to see me. He wouldn't tell me where he was.

The next morning, I called him again and told him I was headed in the direction I knew he was. He again told me not to come. He told me I wouldn't like what he had to say. I didn't tell him that I hadn't liked anything about him for the last four months. I told him I was coming. Finally, he agreed to tell me where he was once I got there. Until then, he would be "working." I asked if he had gotten a job. He said he was going to be shingling a roof. I would find out later that he had gotten a number of a man who needed some shingling done. Nothing would ever come out of it.

And so I left on my four-hour drive. I felt confident that I was doing what God had told me to do. I felt confident this would work. When I left, I told my girls this was my last effort. I had tried everything else. I told them if this didn't work, then I was done. All of this back and forth stuff was hard on the girls, especially Lexi. This had to work.

CHAPTER 22

Disaster

I left confident. I was confident Donnie would tell me where he was once I got down the road. I was right. I was confident we would be able to talk things out, that he would come home, and that maybe he would get some help. I also felt if he didn't get help that he would crash soon and the thought of this happening in the middle of nowhere with no one around to help him scared me. I hadn't forgotten the depression from four years ago. If it hit him, he would not be able to make it home.

Taylor had gone on vacation with Ethan's family. I was happy for her to have a break, yet I hated for her to go. Taylor brought me calmness, and she was smart in her ideas on how to handle her father. I asked her advice often. Kaylee was working and I had Lexi at a friend's house; I began my journey.

It was a four-hour drive. I had called Donnie to tell him I had left. Again, he told me not to come. He reminded me I wouldn't like what he had to say. My confidence kept me driving. Eventually, he told me to call when I pulled into town and he would tell me where to find him. This was a victory, one I had expected. I could see we were playing on his terms.

One thing that I was hoping to find out today was a deep secret, one Donnie had told my girls he would take to his grave. He told them it was something I had done and for the life of me, besides the Diet Coke, I couldn't figure it out. My girls and others Donnie had told kept asking me, and I really didn't have a clue as to what he was talking about.

I arrived and called in the town he had told me to. We were definitely playing on his terms. He told me to drive to the next town and meet at a gas station. As I pulled into this station, I quickly figured out where Donnie had been spending his time. Behind the station was a casino. I saw Donnie standing by his truck and pulled in. He looked tired.

I must have been running on adrenaline. I felt invincible. The first thing I noticed was Donnie did not act one bit glad to see me. And he wouldn't let me touch him. In fact, he told me not to touch him. He suggested we take a walk. He picked a spot by a creek, across from the casino for our talk. I suggested we go down over the hill since so many cars were driving by. He agreed. He jumped the creek and sat across from me, the creek was between us. He reminded me again he did not want me touching him.

I told him I had been doing some soul-searching and praying. I told him God had showed me that I should have gone to Pete's funeral with him. He nodded his head in satisfaction. I talked for probably half an hour, telling him everything I had ever done wrong in our marriage. He looked pleased at my realization. Then he told me I was too late.

He told me a story then. A few days ago, when he was ready to go into the casino, he prayed to God to bring him a woman that would love him the way he deserved to be loved. He said he knew that God did not want him to be alone. Right after that prayer, he met a waitress who took his order. They began talking and got to know each other quite well, it sounded like. He told me that she loved animals just like Donnie did. Donnie has always liked animals, but love might be a stretch. He told me she loved horses just like he did. He also told me that she loved children just like he did. The waitress had told him about her horrible childhood, told him her mother had tried to kill her. Donnie told me that was another thing he and the waitress had in common, a miserable childhood. Donnie said he had told her he was married and she had also given him her phone number.

I listened, not moving, not saying a word. When he was finished, Donnie had one more thing to tell me. What he said next was that this waitress was brought to him by God. He knew she was the one.

I looked at him, and then calmly, I said, "You met a waitress yesterday and you love her?" He said he did. Then I summarized back to him what he had told me. "You prayed to God to bring you a woman. You are a married man, and you think God brought you this woman?" He said yes. Then he told me that she was a Christian, and that is how he knew for sure. Again, I questioned him. "This woman is a Christian and she knows you're married and still gave you her phone number?" Yes, that was right.

I asked him what she was like. He said she was beautiful, not heavy, and not too thin, with long, thick black hair. He said she had the most beautiful eyes he had ever seen. He told me she was twenty-three. That would be the point that I lost it. I became enraged, yet in a calm way. I told him fine, if he wanted to do this to go ahead. I told him that before I left, I wanted him to call some people and tell them himself. I wasn't going to be accused of messing up this story.

He wasn't thrilled with this but was willing. First, I told him to call Tommy. I told him that Tommy and Beth had known I was coming and were waiting to hear. He called. Tommy tried to show him how wrong all of this was, he wouldn't listen.

Next, I told him to call his sister Tammy. He explained everything to her. Tammy was crying and yelling at him, trying to get him to see he was making a mistake. He wouldn't listen. That call didn't end well. He was rattled.

Next, I told him to call Taylor and then Kaylee. He was not willing to do this. I asked if I was supposed to tell them. He said yes, and to make sure I included all the details that I had shared with him about not putting our marriage first. He wasn't about to take the blame.

I had one more question before I left. I was upset but still pretty calm. I asked him about the secret. He told me the same thing he had told my girls. He was going to take that secret to the grave with him.

I climbed the hill. I started to head to the casino. I would march in there and let his new little girlfriend have it, maybe even get her fired. He told me she wasn't working. I turned and went to my vehicle. Before I got in, he told me again to file for divorce. He told me to do it soon; he wanted to get on with his life. He told me he would help with bills and taking care of the girls. I told him it would be expensive to keep two women. He told me that the only thing he wanted was split custody of Lexi.

I got in and spun out of the parking lot. I don't think I have ever screeched my tires in my life. I screeched them for a long ways and more than once. I took one last peek back at Donnie. He stood at his truck and stared.

I started the four-hour drive home. I called my girls and told them. Both were crying and upset. In my mind and according to scripture, Donnie had committed adultery. He had intimate conversations with this woman; he had searched her out and pursued her. He even took her phone number.

It was a long drive home. I stopped a couple of times and took more money out for my stash. I knew now that I had to do something legal to keep him from getting Lexi.

I was convinced this was my last attempt at surviving this hell and coming out okay. I had to get out for my girls' sake and for my own. I didn't know what I was up against; I couldn't fathom what the "secret" was. I knew it was something his sick mind had made up. I knew I had a fight on my hands where Lexi was concerned.

Later, I would find out what happened next in Donnie's story. As soon as I left, he went to see his new love, Jodi. She had told him that she was scared of her ex-boyfriend. He had tried to call her and she didn't answer. He kept trying and became worried. He went to her address. I believe God clearly intervened and kept Donnie from doing something that I would be unable to forgive.

When Donnie found her house and pulled into her drive, he saw a pickup there. He knocked and no one answered. He said he was concerned for Jodi's safety. His paranoia was working at its best. He started to knock on the windows. He said he went next door and questioned the neighbor. The neighbor lady finally told him that she didn't know what he wanted with this girl but to stay away from her. The lady told Donnie he seemed like a nice guy and he didn't want that kind of trouble.

Later that night, Donnie went to the casino. He said he was sitting at the bar drinking when security came up and ask him to go with them. Apparently, he had scared his new little girlfriend when he was beating on her windows. She had turned him in at the casino where she worked and said he was a threat. Donnie was asked to leave the casino and told he couldn't come back. This was a small victory, but the damage was done.

Taylor told Donnie that she didn't want to see him anymore and that if he chose to be with that woman, who was only a few years older than Taylor herself, then she wanted nothing to do with him.

Kaylee began texting her dad Bible verses. She let him know that he had already committed adultery. She also told him she wanted nothing to do with this new girlfriend. Donnie asked both of them if they just wanted him to spend the rest of his life alone.

I never told Lexi about the other woman. Her heart was hurting enough and I didn't want to have to try to help her understand. There was no way for me to tell her without telling her how wretched her dad was in my mind and how much I hated him. I had worked really hard to help Lexi understand yet help her keep loving him like before.

I did just as Donnie told me to do. I owned up to my end of things. I made sure my girls knew that I hadn't always taken good care of our marriage. I also reminded them that I was done trying. They both agreed I had tried enough. The three of us, me, Taylor, and Kaylee decided we would do all we could to keep Lexi out of his hands. Taylor and Kaylee both said they would never speak to Donnie again if he tried to get Lexi.

I wasn't sure what God had tried to tell me. Obviously, I had misunderstood. I had gone so confident that I had heard Him talk to me and tell me to go. I was confident He had told me there would be victory and things would start to get better. I didn't think things could get worse. This had to be rock bottom.

On my way home, I talked to a friend who handed the phone over to someone else. This person told me that they knew my story and that they were sure Donnie was bipolar. They said their spouse was also bipolar. This person gave me a lot of information, scary information. Bipolar isn't something that goes away. The person on the phone told me that by my description Donnie had type one bipolar. This type is the most difficult to convince the patient that they have it. It is next to impossible to get them on medication and keep them on it. This new information didn't really help take away the sting of my latest information. It did, though, give me strength to move forward. One foot in front of the other, breathe, breathe. My head was filled with this and nothing else.

CHAPTER 23

The Secret

B y the next day, I knew the secret. Donnie had shared the fact that he had a secret about me that he would take to his grave with a lot of people. He also had shared the secret with a few, who shared it with a few, who shared it with a few…you get the hint. By the time I got back, the whole town knew my secret and finally someone was willing to tell me.

My dear friend Tasha had someone come to her and ask if Donnie was okay. They had run into Donnie at a Walmart in another town. Right there in the middle of the store, Donnie had shared the secret.

Hold on to your seats and get ready. The horrible, terrible thing I did was have premarital sex. Yes, Donnie and I started dating at age fifteen and we dated and were sexually active with each other all through high school. This is not something I'm proud of, but I didn't become a Christian until age twenty-three. I had already taken care of this with God. It was part of my past. I had only been with Donnie and no one else. I couldn't even imagine it.

In Donnie's very seriously ill mind, I had committed the crime and he was totally innocent. Everyone he had told thought he was nuts. Half the population has premarital sex, why on earth was he slamming me for it if it was with him? No one understood.

When I finally learned of the secret, I just laughed. Surely when he thought this through, he would see the ridiculousness of it. Laughing is good medicine. The relief of the secret being out in the open took some of the edge off of my frayed emotions. I knew there was no way Donnie would ever get custody of Lexi if he tried. I had too many people who knew he was crazy. I told my girls the big secret before they heard it from somebody else. They were not shocked or horrified. They were seriously grossed out and convinced more than ever that their dad had totally lost it.

CHAPTER 24

Prayer Meeting

I was convinced I had heard God wrong. Yet I couldn't press on and file for a divorce and plan to keep Lexi from her dad. God kept showing me that I needed to go to Donnie again. I was flabbergasted. By Sunday morning, I was so distraught that I called Tasha and asked her to invite people to my house to pray after church.

Donnie's sister notified me that Donnie was heading our direction. He was coming home. I was terrified. Donnie had called me that morning. I didn't answer. He was persistent so finally I talked to him. He asked me to meet him again. He was leaving our hometown and asked if I would meet him halfway so we could talk things out without interruption. I told him I would think about it.

A few hours later, the prayer group poured in and filled my living room. Most of them knew what was happening, but for those who didn't, I tried to sum it up for them and shared about Donnie's new love. I fell apart several times and I was relieved that Tommy and Beth were here and were able to tell it for me. I remember Beth saying that I couldn't take anymore.

People began to talk, giving opinions. They tried to suggest ways to get him committed. I told him there was no way to do it. I told them my heart was telling me to go to him again, but my head was telling me no. Several, especially the men in the room, told me I should not go, and if I really felt I had to then I should not go alone. I told them Donnie wouldn't hurt me. They asked me how I could be sure; I hadn't suspected anything that had happened so far. I told them I just knew.

We spent some time in prayer then. I was so mentally and emotionally drained. I just sat and cried. When the prayer ended, there was more planning on what we could do to help Donnie. I explained again and said there is no help until he crashes and helps himself. I looked across from me at Karen. I could tell she was deep in thought. I asked her what she was thinking. I can't remember exactly her words, but to sum it up, she said that all of our planning was human forms of trying to control the situation. This was pointless and had gotten us nowhere. We needed to turn it over to God and beg him to intervene.

We began to pray again. I felt a calmness come over me and I felt my mind was made up. I could clearly hear God telling me to go. When we finished the prayer, Pat said these words: "You should always follow your heart and not your head. Your heart is where God works through you." That was it. My decision was made. I was going. I knew right then that I would not contact my family. They would be totally against my going. I promised to keep in touch. I would let Tommy and Beth know where I was going and when we met up and how it was going along the way.

My girls reminded me that a few days ago, when I went to meet Donnie had been my last effort. They were tired of the back-and-forth business and thought it was time I stopped playing into his sick mind games. I didn't blame them. Part of me wanted to crawl into bed and not go. I knew if I didn't meet up with him, then he would head home, and I didn't want whatever was about to happen to happen in front of the girls.

I left for my second time in a week to meet up with my husband. I felt a tug of hope that maybe he had come to his senses and would agree to get help. If not, then I knew this was it. I couldn't do it anymore.

I felt guilty not letting my family know what was going on. I remember texting my mom and telling her. I told her I knew she wouldn't agree, but I also knew Donnie was sick and I couldn't just walk away if there was a chance of helping him. She texted me back with a cold "It's your life." I didn't contact family members again for a few days. I came to realize that people had no way of understanding. If you hadn't seen it, there was no way to understand it. My family was worried about my well-being as well as the girls'. They couldn't understand why I kept going back and forth. I couldn't really understand it either, other than I loved my husband, and if things never got fixed, I wanted to make sure I had done everything I could. I also knew that this man was not really Donnie. I held out hope that he was still in there somewhere. Lastly, God wouldn't let me walk away, no matter how hard I tried.

CHAPTER 25

Confusion

No surprise, I arrived first by a good half hour. I knew this would happen as Donnie was easily sidetracked these days. I parked at a convenience store and got out and walked to the far end of the parking lot. I never stopped praying. There were wild daisies growing there. I did something silly and picked one and pulled off the petals one by one, saying, "He loves me, he loves me not." I came up short and found that he loved me not. I did it again for good measure. He still loved me not. I tossed the flowers.

Donnie pulled in, canoe strapped to the top. He got out and I walked toward him. I still had the sting of him telling me not to touch him a few days before. I kept my distance and stopped quite a ways from him. He walked to me, grabbed me, and hugged me tight. I was speechless and confused. He asked me to get in and ride with him to a nearby park so we could walk and talk. I'm not going to lie, it did cross my mind that he was going to take me into the woods, kill me, and dispose of the body in a lake somewhere. I was scared yet I felt God with me, telling me to go.

I went and didn't get much relief when we pulled into a lake. So this is where they would eventually find my body? My mind was working overtime. Donnie was nothing but kind. His eyes were different than they had been a few days ago. The wild, glassy look was gone. He still looked tired, but the more I looked at his eyes, the more I could see him in there. I knew I had made the right decision.

We talked. He apologized for the other day. He told me the story of Jodi and how she had him banned from the casino. Donnie told me that he felt Jodi was a test. In fact, he didn't know if she was really even a person. He told me he had been wrong and confused, and he now realized that when he prayed to God to bring him a woman that God sent me the next day.

We talked for hours; we put the canoe in the lake and paddled around. Donnie had told me to bring an overnight bag so that we didn't have to rush, so we had plenty of time to talk. I did and we planned to stay until the following day. Donnie never admitted there was anything wrong with him, other than being confused. He felt we had some issues in our marriage that we needed to work out. I told him I didn't trust him anymore, not after Jodi. He said he understood. We talked a lot about ways we could take time for each other and not always put the girls first.

CHAPTER 26

Get Out of the Boat

The next day, Donnie asked me to go canoeing with him in the Missouri River. Something I haven't shared yet is that I can't swim and I am terrified of the water. I've had two bad water experiences that left me scared to death of drowning. The last thing I wanted to do was get in a canoe with someone I was trying to trust again. I didn't want to ruin things, they were going pretty well. I agreed.

Since we had two vehicles, we parked one at a bridge then drove down the road several miles to unload the canoe. We figured it would take us a couple of hours to canoe to our other vehicle.

We got in and the water was calm. I began to feel calm too. I also felt God prodding me to do this, no matter how scared I was, no matter how much I really did not want to do it.

We paddled out maybe a football field away from the shore. We pulled out our paddles and sat across from each other. We were discussing how this should all happen, how long it would take. We took in the beauty around us. The sandbanks were soft white sand like I had never seen before. The river stretched as far as we could see both ways. I began to relax.

I will do my best to tell you what happened next. We sat there, oars out of the water, water so calm it looked like a mirror, the air perfectly still. All of a sudden, I was airborne. The canoe flipped upside down. I didn't go under like I should have with the canoe tipping. Instead, I was thrown from the canoe in one direction, Donnie in the other. My head never went under water. I landed softly. My only explanation for what happened is that God threw us out of that boat.

It took me a minute to get my bearings. Once I did, I began to panic. I quickly remembered that I couldn't swim. I was in very deep water. My life jacket was keeping me afloat. Donnie immediately began to talk to me; I couldn't see him as he was on the other side of the canoe. I was frozen. Donnie had to get the canoe turned over on his own. I was having trouble breathing. It was becoming harder and harder to get a breath.

Once he got the canoe flipped over, Donnie told me we would have to work together to get in the canoe. We were far from shore. I am glad that Donnie didn't mention the huge fish that could have swallowed my toes whole. It didn't even cross my mind. Later, when I would see the fish jumping and see how big they were, let's just say I was glad not to figure this out until we were back in the boat.

Donnie told me I would have to trust him to help me back in the canoe. I told him I couldn't move and I couldn't breathe. He talked me into inching my way over to the canoe. I grabbed a hold of it. He was on the other side and told me to let go of the canoe and grab his hands. My hands were glued to that canoe. I couldn't make them let go. Terror had paralyzed me. He kept talking to me calmly. I would find out later that he was well aware of the large fish and was trying to hurry me along before I discovered them and freaked out.

I finally grabbed Donnie's hands. Using himself as a counterweight, he pulled me into the boat. Then I held on for dear life as he rocked the canoe getting himself back in. We sat there shaking and wet. Then we looked at each other and asked what had just happened. Neither of us had gone under, both of us had gone airborne in opposite directions, and we had accomplished the near impossible and gotten ourselves back in the boat.

By now, we were even farther from shore. We pressed on and stopped on one of the sand dunes so I could calm down and get it together. We kept playing over in our minds what had happened and came to the only conclusion there was. God had thrown us out of that boat. We had to trust each other to get ourselves back in.

Once we were calm, we decided to continue on our journey. When we parked the vehicles, we forgot to think about the twists and turns in the river. The two hours we thought it would take turned into ten hours. We had eaten breakfast but had planned to have lunch after our trip. That night at ten o'clock, we finally ate and drank.

We were exhausted, but looking back, God was totally with us on that trip. Later, we would talk to a couple who does a lot of canoeing. They were shocked that we even attempted to canoe on a large river. They said it is very difficult and they never do it. We had no food with us and very little water. We weren't prepared and it was hot.

The water did not remain calm, it became rougher in spots. Never once did our canoe tip or even act like it was going to capsize again. In the whole ten hours, we saw three fishermen on the bank, and one boat passed us. That was it.

I had hoped to get Donnie in that canoe in the middle of nowhere and do some talking. That didn't happen. He avoided all conversation that had anything to do with him being ill. But still, God was on that boat with us. I didn't accomplish the things that I wanted to, but it was not in vain.

When we headed home the next day, we had a great story to tell of how God had thrown us out of the boat. For the first time in four months, I had some hope. Donnie wasn't here all the time, but I started to see glimpses of him. Other people would talk to him and tell me that it was like at times, he was coming out of his illness. Maybe the crash didn't have to happen after all.

CHAPTER 27

Crazy Woman

D onnie wanted us to travel often, just the two of us. I always felt like he was testing me to see if I would leave the girls and pick him over them. I was scared not to these days. I had decided the girls were safer with him gone, so if that meant me going with him, I would do it. Taylor and Kaylee were old enough to handle things with me gone, but Lexi was really starting to suffer from the frequent absence of her parents.

Donnie asked me to go away for the weekend again. He reminded me that we needed time for us. He had an area in mind. He needed to speak with some of the Native Americans at the casino we had stayed at before. He said God was telling him he needed to go before the tribal council and ask them to "fund" some of his business opportunities and work out a way that they also would benefit from this.

I had become a crazy woman. I don't know why, but I agreed. We planned to go and then take a little side trip and go watch my nieces play softball in the state tournament. Remember, I was crazy by this point, so I don't remember much about this trip. His talk with the Native Americans consisted of small talk at the hotel desk.

I also remember Donnie asking me to go gambling with him. I didn't want to at all. He kept pushing, saying that he wanted me to see what he does in the casinos, how he shined for Jesus as he gambled away all of our money. I finally agreed to go. Before he started, he told me that if he didn't do well today with me there, then he would know it was a sign from God to stop gambling.

I hate the atmosphere of casinos. First of all, the smoke makes me sick. Second of all, I think it is sad to see so many old or disabled people trying to grow their fixed incomes at the slot machines. It seemed to me that most people there were glassy eyed and intoxicated. I'm not trying to sound judgmental. Casinos just are not for me. But I went to watch my husband do his thing.

He played a few slots and lost everything he put in. He then hit the blackjack tables. He asked me to sit on his right side and to touch him at all times. What was I, some kind of lucky charm? He played with confidence, and as the night went on, I watched him blow over $500. I told him I'd had enough. He said he was just getting started. I told him I was leaving and would see him in the truck. He was in the casino for another couple of hours. He lost a lot of money, I know that. He told me he didn't win anything and that maybe he wasn't supposed to gamble anymore. I decided if that was what came out of it, then maybe it wasn't in vain.

The next day, we went to watch my nieces play ball. On the drive there, Donnie began to hound me about reaching out to Toby and his girlfriend. I want you to know right now that I like them. That isn't why I didn't want to reach out to them. I tried to explain to Donnie that my plate was full and running over. I told him with everything going on between us that I had nothing left to give anyone. He kept pushing. He soon became angry and said that I was holding him back from what God was telling him to do. He told me I was like an anchor pulling him under, holding him under.

I became angry. I don't remember the details, but I remember telling Donnie to pull over. I told him I'd had enough. I had listened to him belittle me for over an hour and I couldn't take it anymore. I told him that if he didn't pull over, I would jump out of the truck. He pulled over.

This is another one of those times that I'm not proud of. I felt like I had literally gone crazy. I grabbed my debit card and started walking in the opposite direction. We were on a highway in the middle of nowhere. Donnie tore out and turned around. He was driving on the wrong side of the road with traffic coming. I told him to leave me alone, I couldn't do it anymore. Again, I turned in the opposite direction he was going.

Next thing I know, Donnie had gone down in the ditch with his truck and was following me. I finally turned down a gravel road. If I had driven upon an incident like this, I would have called the police. It had to look like Donnie was stalking and harassing me. If the police would have come, we probably would have both been hauled in. At one point, Donnie pulled up beside me on the gravel road. He asked me where I was going. I told him I didn't know, just away from him. He got out of the truck, left it running, left his door open, and started walking. So here we were both walking in the opposite direction, truck idling in the road. I finally caved. I went back to the truck and told him to get in. I was crying and told him to drive me to the nearest ER. I wanted to commit myself. I was acting and feeling like a crazy woman. I couldn't think, I couldn't focus, and I couldn't breathe.

Donnie agreed I was the one who needed help. He asked me if I was sure I wanted to commit myself. He would take me if that was what I really wanted. I remember at that time feeling so tired that I couldn't move. I was drained. The thought of being committed and away from Donnie for a time was very appealing. In fact, it sounded like a vacation.

Donnie said to me, "What about the girls?" That was all it took. I was slapped back to reality. I couldn't commit myself and leave my girls in Donnie's care. Off to the ball game, we went. I dried my tears, and we watched the game and acted like the perfect all-American couple. When it was over, we headed home.

CHAPTER 28

Full Circle

It was relay time again. Four years ago is when this all started. Four years ago, I survived and said I would never do it again. Now, here I was, reliving the nightmare, only this time, it was worse.

I continued to see glimpses of Donnie. The mania remained. He wasn't working steady and was focused on starting his own businesses again. Notice I said businesses and not business. He had about four irons in the fire. Donnie wanted to buy an existing business, become partners with another small business that was just starting, start his own handyman service, and start another business that he was exploring. It was exhausting and unrealistic. I don't even believe it was possible; maybe one, but not four or even two. He was becoming frustrated that individuals and even the bank would not give him the money.

But still, there were those glimpses. I had to keep trying. I was running on empty, the exhaustion of surviving each day almost too much to handle. I had nothing left for relay. I had done little to contribute this year. It was all I could do to remember to take another breath.

Kaylee had been very ill. She was horribly misdiagnosed at the clinic here in town. Because of this, because proper testing was not done, she had become very sick. Not only was she misdiagnosed, but no testing had even been done to support this diagnosis. We got a second opinion and found the problem, but not before she had gotten very sick. A very simple illness that could have been detected and treated with one simple test; this was very frustrating and added to the already stressed-out household. Remember, what was stressful to me and the girls was intensified by a lot with Donnie and his euphoric behavior. He was beyond upset.

The weather was not cooperating this year for Relay. Because of rain and storms, we were forced to move Relay inside at the last minute. Donnie had promised to come help set up. He never showed and I wasn't surprised. By the time Relay started, I had no clue where he was.

The night dragged on, I had no family there at this important event except for Lexi. Kaylee was sick and Taylor was home with her. I had no clue where Donnie was. Relay is always sad for me, reminds me of my dad, but this year I seemed overwhelmed with sadness. As I sat and watched people, I realized I was lonely. I was tired of doing everything by myself while Donnie was out helping everyone else.

My favorite part of Relay is the lighting of the luminaries honoring the cancer survivors and remembering those who have lost the battle. The names on the luminary bags are read and then a survivor lap is done. Once Relay has started, it mostly runs itself until the lighting of the bags.

I had lit a couple of bags when Donnie appeared. He looked very upset and said he needed to talk to me now. It wasn't a good time. I needed to be helping for the next few minutes. I looked in his eyes. They were wild; he wasn't there. I knew I had to go with him then or there would be a scene. I passed off my lighter to someone else and followed him. Nothing could have prepared me for what I was about to hear.

CHAPTER 29

The Beginning of the End

I've already told you Donnie was struggling with his childhood with unresolved issues with his dad. His feelings were justified, but he had always ignored things until the euphoric behavior. Now the pain of the past was intensified and taking over his thoughts and emotions.

Donnie felt he had reached out to his dad. He felt he had only received the leftovers that his dad had to give after giving all of his time and attention to his stepchildren and stepgrandchildren. This is something that had irritated me since I had known Donnie. Donnie wasn't making this up, it was very noticeable and our girls had also suffered and received the leftovers. We had tried talking to his dad and stepmom many times about this, but there was never any improvement.

Donnie was so upset about Kaylee's illness, not only the misdiagnosis but also how it had been handled and how she had been treated when she was seeing the doctor. He had a right to be upset, what had happened was outrageous, but it was affecting him in a bad way. He called his dad, sharing what had happened with Kaylee. From what I understand, he asked his dad and stepmom to come. The way Donnie explained things to me, his dad and stepmom were at his brother's for his son's birthday. Then they were heading on to their vacation. Donnie said he had asked them to stop by after leaving the party and before going on vacation.

The answer was no. They said maybe they could stop after vacation. Donnie told them that Kaylee was very sick and would appreciate a visit. What Donnie didn't understand was that Kaylee was sick enough that she did not want company. Because they had not stayed in contact, even though several people had told them Donnie was sick and needed help, they were not seeing his cry for help. Donnie wanted his dad. Just like other times in his life that he was wanting his dad, his dad didn't make an effort to come.

Outside of the building where Relay was being held, Donnie told me this, crying. He then told me that he had called his stepmom and told her he was tired of the leftovers. He told her to tell his dad that he was ending their relationship. Donnie told me then that Ike, his stepdad who raised him, had really been Donnie's only father. Donnie had Ike on a high pedestal and rightly so. He told me he was going to change his last name to Crawford. He told me that he felt much relief to have finally removed the knife from his back that had continually cut and wounded him over and over. He told me he forgave his dad, but he was done with them.

I was speechless. All the disagreements I had with those in-laws in the past, all the times they had angered me to the point of boiling over, all the times I had watched them hurt Donnie and my girls, I thought I would be glad. But I wasn't. I told Donnie I was sorry and that we would talk more right after Relay. I had to get back in to help with what was going on. He told me okay.

I didn't see him again until the end of Relay. As we were cleaning up, he came. He didn't look at me, he didn't speak to me. He stayed and visited but did nothing to help. There was no reason for him to be there if he wasn't helping. I began to shake. I knew by his wild eyes that something bad was about to happen. I was right.

I struggled to carry a large box to my vehicle as I was leaving. Donnie came up beside me. I asked him where his truck was. He told me he had the four-wheeler parked a ways away. I told him to get in and I would give him a ride to it. I told him we could talk about what happened with his dad.

Once again, his anger was very controlled, yet so vicious. I was scared. He told me that he had needed me again, and I had chosen Relay. I was always choosing something else over him. I kept my cool, but all I could think was how he was never around for our family anymore because he was always trying to help someone else.

Before he walked away from me, he said something to me that chilled me to the bone. It wasn't really what he said, but the controlled venomous anger that he said it with. He said, "I will never choose you over God." Then he walked away.

CHAPTER 30

Terror

I got home and waited for Donnie to show up. After thirty minutes, I texted him to see when he would be home. He told me he was visiting with a young man. I asked him if he was at the kid's house. He told me he was visiting with him at the bar. I asked him to come home. He told me no.

I waited up for a long time. I finally went to bed around 2:00 a.m. Donnie hadn't yet been home. I had just fallen asleep when he abruptly woke me up. I was startled when he grabbed the blankets and pulled them back and told me to get out of bed. This was close to four or five a.m. I could smell alcohol and smoke. What happened next is somewhat of a blur. I remember Donnie standing over me as I sat in our living room. He wasn't drunk but had definitely been drinking. He looked like the devil was spewing out of him. That is the only way I can describe it. I was scared.

He told me that he had poured his heart out to me about his dad and I hadn't cared. I tried to explain to him that I had an obligation and I left to talk to him and then he told me we would talk after. He then went on a tangent, bashing Relay, saying how lame it was, how stupid it was, how no one liked it. I ignored him.

He towered over me as he told me again that he would *never* choose me over God. All the things he was doing were direct orders from God. He told me I either get on board or he was done. I waited for him to hit me. I had never been so sure that it would happen. He had his fists balled, and I knew I was going to be hit in the face. I was shaking uncontrollably.

I then realized that he had no right to do what he was doing. In my eyes, he was a lunatic. I calmly told him to get out until he got help. This opened another whole can of rage for him. How dare I kick him out when he had just lost his dad. I told him that had been his choice, his decision. I told him I was not going to put up with him going to the bars. He told me people accepted him there, were glad to see him. He told me the people in the bars were just like him, they didn't have a lot of love from their dads growing up and had been wounded in the same ways he had. He called the people in the bar down-and-outers and said he fit in there, he was liked there. He told me the whole time he was there he was preaching about Jesus.

Then I made a big mistake. I asked him who would listen to him preaching about Jesus while he was pouring beer down his throat. I could see a beast in him then and I knew it was time to be done. I asked him again to get out. He threatened me one more time, telling me he would never give up Lexi. He told me to file for divorce the next day. Then he slammed the door and left. I sat shaking for a long time. There was no way to keep him out; he could get in whenever he wanted. I was terrified. I had never seen him so angry, out of control, yet controlled. It is hard to explain. He told me everything was coming from God, but to me, it looked like Satan had his hands wrapped tight around Donnie's throat.

CHAPTER 31

Class Reunion

The next day, Donnie returned. I don't know why I kept caving, kept staying with a man I was so scared of. My only guess is that we had a twenty-five–year class reunion coming up and also our twenty-fifth wedding anniversary. Twenty-five years thrown out the window is a huge waste. I know in my heart I wanted to save my marriage. I also believe Donnie did too. So we were trying our best to reconcile.

We decided to make a weekend of our class reunion. I was weary to go. I knew Donnie had run his mouth in our hometown and it had gotten back to me that some of our classmates had heard from Donnie we were getting a divorce.

We were the couple who dated all through high school, got married right after graduation, the couple everyone was shocked was still together at the five-, ten-, and twenty-year reunions. I wasn't looking forward to going, not to mention Donnie's behavior.

We went, I survived. We actually had a pretty good time. We got along until later into the evening when I asked Donnie to slow down on the drinks. He joked about it there, but when we left, he was angry. I didn't realize this until we walked out and I asked for the keys to drive. He told me he was perfectly capable of driving. He threw the keys at me and got in. He was furious and verbally unleashed his anger in the truck as I was driving.

By the time we got to the hotel, he was raging. I began to get angry. He had been drinking too much, everyone was talking about it. I wanted to vomit, listening to him talk about how great he was and how much he loved Jesus. People at the reunion were starting to laugh and talk about him being drunk. The more he drank, the louder he got, and when you are having manic behavior, your volume level is already maxed out.

So we fought. Anger came out of me that I had bottled up for months. I told him that was it, drink all you want, smoke all you want, I'm done. I tried to leave the hotel room. He blocked the door.

This chapter is hard to write. It is not a proud moment for me by a long shot. I have no excuse for my behavior other than I had lost it. I had finally been pushed over the edge. I was tired, tired, tired. I was mad at myself for going back to him over and over again. I was mad that I had to go through this again. Most of all, I was mad at God. The madder I got, the more Donnie started to shrink up like an abused animal, totally playing the victim. I had had it.

I tried again to leave and Donnie restrained me from getting to the door. That was the last straw. I started to punch him and I bit him. On the shoulder, I left a full set of teeth marks. All of my pent-up rage was coming out. I needed out of that room. I felt like a caged animal and I had to get out. He let go of me when I bit him but still blocked the door. I ran for the phone to call 911. He stopped me again. He told me that he would be hauled off, arrested. He told me the police would believe me over him and he wouldn't stand a chance of not being put in jail. That was my chance, but I couldn't do it.

I fell on the bed, sobbing, and asked Donnie to take me to a mental facility. I told him I couldn't do it anymore. There he was. He was back. I could see it in his eyes. He had pity for me. He said he would take me and help me get committed, but before I decided for sure, I needed to think of the girls. Again, that was all it took to snap me back to reality. If I committed myself, my girls would have no one but this lunatic to take care of them. I curled up and fell asleep.

From here, things spun out of control again. Donnie couldn't stay out of the bars and I didn't want to live my life that way. My girls rarely saw their dad and they were glad. Yet he was always lurking.

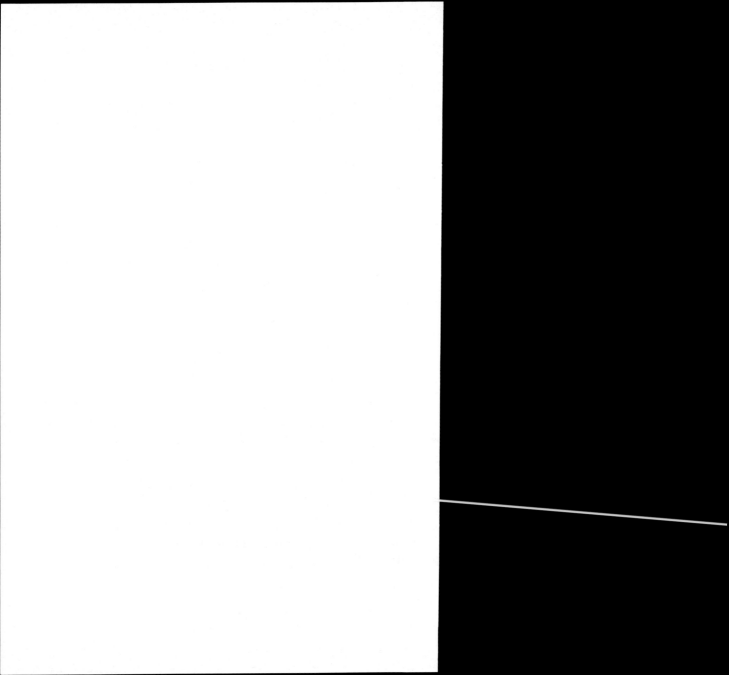

CHAPTER 32

Bars

Shortly after the night of Relay, the night he disowned his dad, Donnie received a letter in the mail from his stepmom. I didn't open it when it came, but let Donnie know it was here. After he read it, I read it and it made me cry. It was a cruel letter. I knew that it was written by people that had been hurt by Donnie's actions. But they had also caused pain and they had been told over and over by several people that Donnie was sick. I didn't understand how anybody could send a letter like that to someone they knew was ill and not in control of their actions. Donnie was crushed even more than he had been. He did not respond to the letter, but I noticed big changes after he got it.

Every night, Donnie went to the bars. He hung out with a lot of Taylor's friends. They filled the bars as they were just turning twenty-one. Taylor would get texts from her friends at the bar, telling her they were hanging out with her dad and how cool he was. Finally, Kaylee came to me and said, "Mom, that's enough. You have put up with enough, no one else would put up with that much. You need to kick Dad out for good." Kaylee had always stuck up for her dad, four years ago, and even now she always tried to give him the benefit of the doubt. Her words gave me the courage to do what I should have done a long time ago.

I gave Donnie an ultimatum. I told him to stop the bars or get out. He chose the bars because that is what God was telling him to do. He reminded me again that I was an anchor holding him down.

Donnie moved into the basement of a family across the street. Kaylee was horrified as this was one of her classmate's. It wasn't nearly far enough away for me. Donnie came the next morning, calmer, but still angry. In his eyes, he was the victim. He told Lexi he would be across the street and that she could stay with him sometimes. He told her he had the basement to himself and she could come and play there whenever she wanted. Then, on his way out the door, he told me to keep this between us. He said the town was already talking, and he didn't want to give people anything more to talk about.

I watched him go. I felt no relief. He was too close. I wasn't about to let Lexi go over there without me or her sisters. I shouldn't have worried. Donnie never took the time to have her come. He was too busy helping everyone else in our town. As for keeping this between us, he told everyone he saw that I kicked him out. He played the victim well. He never told anyone why I kicked him out, just that I had.

I didn't sleep much these days so when I was up at night I would look out the window and never once did I see his truck in the driveway at night. He would usually roll in around 5 a.m. I would see his truck at the bar. At first, it would be there around 8, then it became 7, and then it became 5 p.m. Once on our way to the pool, Lexi saw her dad's truck at the bar. Her eyes filled with tears and she asked why her daddy would go bowling without her. I explained to her that he wasn't bowling, that he was at the bar, not the bowling alley. She tried to convince herself that he was bowling because the bar was connected to the bowling alley. I guess she finally decided it hurt less to have him at the bar than to have him bowling without her. We saw his truck there often, but she never questioned it again.

Donnie became involved with a couple of guys who were what he would call, down-and-outers. They both suffered from depression and drug use. They both convinced Donnie they wanted and needed his help. They both used and abused Donnie's kindness and took terrible advantage of him.

Donnie continued to hit the bars every night. He would brag to everyone how he was there witnessing to people. He would tell me how he was treated better there than anywhere. He was convinced the people at the bars really cared about him. He also made frequent trips out of town to casinos. I could easily track this by our bank account.

One day, Donnie asked to take Lexi to lunch. I let him. I wasn't worried at the time about him taking her. He was all talk; he didn't want to be tied down at night. How would he go to the bars if he had to worry about Lexi? When they left, Lexi made him promise that he wasn't taking her to the bar. They went to Subway that day and Donnie came back very excited. He said he had met a prophet. Apparently, he and Lexi had stumbled upon a man, a very smelly, dirty man. The man was upset that he couldn't get a sandwich, something about his debit card not working. So Donnie did what any crazy man would do. He bought the guy lunch and had his eight-year-old daughter eat with a complete stranger.

Donnie told me how knowledgeable the man was of the Bible. Donnie said he was down on his luck. The cashier at Subway told Donnie he should stay away from the guy, that he had been causing trouble around town. This was a great encouragement to Donnie. One more jewel in his crown for helping someone that everyone else was disgusted by. How could he have Lexi around this man after hearing the warnings?

Lexi told me later that she had been very uncomfortable around the man. Donnie had told Lexi they would try to find the guy in the park later. I told Lexi she was never to go near him again, even with her dad. Lexi agreed that he was scary and that she should not be around him.

Later, I found out that the police had finally taken him in. He was on bipolar and other mental disorder medications, which he had not been taking. Since he was not taking his medication, by the time they escorted him out of town, he was becoming threatening. It terrified me that Donnie had subjected Lexi to this. He had encouraged her to befriend this man. After I filled Donnie in on this new information, he said that he had figured out the guy wasn't a prophet. He said that the things he was saying were confusing and anyone talking about Jesus should not sound confusing. I instantly pictured Donnie in the bar, pouring beer down his throat and talking to people about Jesus. I made no comment.

I held it together, that is all I accomplished each day. I did what I could to comfort Lexi. She didn't want to spend time with her dad; she was scared of him and felt rejected by him. There was one instance where Donnie hadn't seen her for quite a while. Lexi decided to ask him to go swimming again. Kaylee was a lifeguard, and I knew she would notify me if I needed to come to the pool. A few hours before they were to go, Donnie stopped by the house and told Lexi something important had come up and he would have to cancel their swimming date. I found out the next day that polka dancing with strangers was more important to Donnie than his daughter. The few times he did go, Lexi would end up swimming alone while Donnie played with all the other children at the pool, leaving her out.

He felt God was directing him to reach out to the kids who had hard lives. That is fine, but Donnie was giving Lexi no attention and her life was becoming harder every day.

Another day, Donnie came to the house and asked me to talk to him in the garage. I went out and was instantly trembling. He told me he was tired of being alone and that he wanted to move on with his life. He asked me to go with him to the courthouse and end our marriage. He said he wanted nothing but half custody of Lexi. I looked at him in disbelief. I told him you couldn't just walk in the courthouse and end twenty-four years of marriage just like that. Then I reminded him that he was not going to get any kind of custody of Lexi.

He remained calm and then asked to talk to Lexi in the garage. I came in and got Lexi. In front of Donnie, I told Lexi to tell her dad the truth. Then I came in. I would find out later that Donnie asked Lexi if she wanted to live with him part of the time. I have already told you Lexi is wise beyond her years. She told her dad she didn't want to leave her sisters but not to worry. She said she would be spending so much time with him that it would be even better than if she lived with him part of the time. This seemed to satisfy him.

He did talk to Lexi about him and me going to the courthouse for a divorce that day. Lexi came in and said that she thought it would be better for us to do that than to drag things out. Donnie had told her how painful it would be for her if that is how we did it. I explained that it wasn't possible. I went to the garage angry and told Donnie if he wanted the divorce then go file but to stop putting Lexi in the middle. I knew he wouldn't file.

It angered me that Donnie was putting Lexi in the middle with this issue. He was using scare tactics with her and I was mad. I confronted him, which in turn made him mad. That is when he threatened me that he would no longer give me any support. He would make sure I got nothing. He told me I better start looking for a job. At the time, I was substitute teaching, but it was summer, so I wasn't working at all. I told him again that if he wanted to file then do it. He told me I would be sorry. He said he would tell the lawyer my dirty little secret. I looked at him, shaking, and asked him if he was going to tell the secret that I had premarital sex with him when we were young. He said yes, he was, and because of what I had done, I would never get custody of Lexi. This didn't scare me, he sounded like a lunatic, and nothing made sense. I did decide then to go job searching. He was telling me he would give me nothing and he had already proved that. We had no income.

Throughout this time, I was running on survival mode alone. It was very much a time of confusion. One minute, Donnie would be asking for a divorce, the next he would be asking me to renew our vows. I remembered that four years ago, he had also pushed me to renew our vows. I could barely process everything and keep it straight. People often tried to encourage me by telling me God wouldn't give me more than I could handle. I was beginning to wonder if God had lost his mind. Exactly what did He think I was made of? I was tired and strung out. I had had it.

This cycle continued for several weeks. Donnie bar-hopped and the whole town knew it. When he went to one bar, he went to all three in town. Sometimes, he bar-hopped out of town. He visited the casinos in nearby towns often. I continued to put one foot in front of the other wondering how I would survive.

CHAPTER 33

Date Night

Donnie came to me a few days later and asked to speak to me in the garage again. He again pushed me to go with him to the courthouse to end our marriage. I told him I wasn't interested. He had caught me on a day when I was feeling stronger and calmer. He asked me if I had gotten a job. I told him I had gotten one and could start when I wanted, I had another one in the works and school would start soon so I would be subbing again. This was all true and so far it sounded like I could work all three jobs without conflict and Taylor and Kaylee could help with Lexi. Donnie acted like he was happy for me, but I could tell it was a knife in his back.

Donnie then told me that he had been thinking and that there were four women that he was interested in pursuing, but he couldn't until I filed for the divorce. I instantly went into the coping mechanism of making my heart hard. Nothing was going to hurt me today.

I asked him who the women were. He told me I knew all of them and he didn't want to tell me, he said he didn't want to hurt me. Really? I played into his little game. I remained calm and interested. I could tell he was dying to tell me. I pushed again, and it all flew out of his mouth. Each had a name and was someone I knew. Two of the four were very young and two more his age. I will not name names now; I have promised Donnie never to do that. But I will tell you what he told me. As he told me about each of them, he stated why he wanted to pursue them, told me of the qualities that were attractive to him, and pretty much pointed out what they had that I was lacking.

Girl number 1 was young and beautiful on the inside and the outside. She was still young enough to have children and Donnie wanted more children. I found this ironic since he was paying little attention to the three he had, not to mention he'd had a vasectomy several years ago.

Girl number 2 I knew well. She was also young enough for more children and she loved sports as much as Donnie did. Girl number 3 was a friend of mine. Donnie already loved her children so it would be a perfect fit. And girl number 4. She loved to smile and have fun. Then Donnie went on to tell me that he had someone picked out for me to pursue as well.

I wanted to vomit. I told him then that even if things didn't work out between us, I had no desire to pursue anyone.

That day in the garage was one of those days when I could catch glimpses of Donnie. Everything he said cut me to the quick. But I remained calm, which helped Donnie remain calm. Next, Donnie told me about his adventures from the night before.

Donnie had gone bar-hopping in another town. This string of bars was known for its wild atmosphere. First, he told me about some kind of secret club. Apparently, only privileged people got in and Donnie was one of the lucky ones. He said once he got in there, God had told him something bad was going on in the place. Apparently, Donnie stayed for a while and soaked in this evil atmosphere. Once he left, he went to the police station in that town to let them know of the evil going on in the place. He told me he talked to the police and told them that since he had gotten in the people trusted him. He told them he could do some undercover work for them. Hmm, now, Donnie had something new to tell everyone. He was going to be doing undercover police work.

I stifled my giggles. I was actually enjoying this. I was invincible today. I asked him if he had to have some special kind of training to do undercover police work. Apparently, he was qualified.

Next, Donnie went on to tell me he had danced the night away. He assured me he mostly danced with older women. I noticed his wedding ring was missing and asked him if he had taken it off before he went dancing. He admitted he had. He also told me that he had gone up onstage with the live band. They had given him a microphone and he sang with them for several hours. He told me he was very good and that the band had asked him back tonight.

So he was going back. I didn't really care at this point. Then Donnie surprised me by inviting me to go. He wanted me to go and enjoy myself, being free to dance with whomever I wanted and watch him do the same. And he wanted me to hear him sing onstage and see how good he was. I had to admit, the curiosity was getting the best of me. Donnie made up a lot of stories, not really on purpose, and he believed all of them. I was curious to see if he really had gotten up to sing with the band. I agreed to go, though I told him I would not be dancing with anyone, but he could feel free to carry on however he wanted.

That was it. I was going crazy again. My moments of sanity were becoming far and few between. I had just agreed to go bar hopping with my husband so that he and I could watch each other dance with other people, pretending we weren't married. I was making myself sick. But just the same, I went.

I got ready, and of course, Donnie was late picking me up. His excuse was that he couldn't leave until he had graced all three bars in town with his presence.

The night was interesting to say the least. Donnie told me to take off my ring. His was already off. I told him I would not. That must have made him feel guilty; he reached in his pocket and pulled out his wedding ring and put it back on his finger. We arrived. First, Donnie had drinks at the bar while we waited for the band to start.

When we heard the band and walked across the dance floor to find a table, I quickly learned Donnie had not been fibbing. The singer announced Donnie by name and said he hoped Donnie would join him onstage again that night. The band played while we sat and listened. I wasn't impressed. Every song was filthy, vulgar, and inappropriate in my book. Donnie looked a bit embarrassed and said that last night they had sung Garth Brooks most of the night.

I watched people dancing. I hadn't been dancing since college, and I have to admit I was pretty appalled. I asked Donnie if that is how he had danced the night away the night before, grinding away, with whoever came near him, man or woman. I was sickened. He told me no.

We danced one slow song together. Donnie then decided it was not the same atmosphere as the night before and that maybe we should go for a walk. We did that and then went back to the bars. It was a long night. As we drove away from it, I knew that if that was the kind of lifestyle Donnie wanted to lead, there was no chance for us. I don't judge people for doing those things; I just know it isn't for me. It didn't used to be for Donnie either, but apparently, he had become bored with his husband-daddy role. That included being the breadwinner.

We had gone with the understanding that this was a date. Donnie dropped me off at home and went who knows where.

That is when I knew that I had to end this. He didn't want to change. He was content going to the bars. I knew he was sick, but I couldn't live this way.

Donnie continued to live across the street. He continued to go to the bars and casinos each night. He also continued to go dancing often. I had asked him over and over to stop. After our date night, we seemed to get along better for a few days. He would stop by more, but then would leave for the bars at 5. I decided he couldn't have it both ways. I needed to be done, if not for me, then for Lexi.

Donnie had made me a copper bracelet. He had given it to me once when we were reconciled for a few days. The night I decided I had had enough, I got up the courage to walk in the bar. I knew he was there and I drove around for an hour trying to get up the courage to go in and end it. I finally did. I walked in and saw him right by the door. He immediately lit up and asked me to come meet his friends. I told him I was done and gave him back the bracelet he had made me.

The next day, I called an attorney. I knew this guy had a reputation for being vicious on deadbeat husbands. I made an appointment and filled him in on what was going on. I had an appointment for the following Friday. He told me it was urgent that I come quickly before Donnie drained the last of our bank account.

There. It was done. The appointment was set and this would all be over soon. The attorney said I would probably have to keep Lexi completely away from Donnie for a while until things were settled. He promised me he would not have any problem accomplishing this. I felt sick.

When I hung up from the lawyer, I dialed another number. Denny and Erma had given me their son's number. He was a family counselor, and I knew Donnie respected him greatly. I cried as I told Chad what was going on and I asked him if he would invite Donnie to come for counseling, the two of us. In my mind, I knew that if Donnie suggested it to me and it looked like his idea that I could get him to go.

I was mad at myself. Everyone was telling me to walk away. Why couldn't I just do it? Maybe it was because I had never asked God. When was the last time I had prayed? Daily, I would beg God to help me, to protect my girls. I needed to turn things over to God and stop taking them back. That is what I did. Right there in a parking lot where I had gone to make phone calls, I gave all of my messy life to God and told Him to handle it. I didn't want to any more.

CHAPTER 34

CMA

When I say CMA, I am not talking about the Country Music Awards. I am talking about the Christian Motorcycle Association. I can hardly wait to tell you how they saved my life one day.

I had asked God to handle things and I guess he did. Within the next few days, Donnie came to me and told me Chad had called him. I had been right. I had begged Donnie to go to counseling, but he wouldn't because I suggested it. This time though, Chad had invited him and Donnie came to me thinking it was his idea. He didn't act very thrilled about it. He acted almost disappointed that he was willing to give our marriage one more shot, but he told me if I was willing to give it a try, then he was too.

Chad and Carma lived about three and a half hours away from us, and Donnie said they could see us the next day. This was hard to explain to my girls. They were tired of me giving their dad chance after chance, tired of me crying all the time, tired of the havoc he was creating in their lives, and tired of seeing no change on his part. I promised them again that this was it. This was my very last attempt. I gave them my word. I had to do the same with my family and also with Tommy and Beth. I had already made these promises and broken them. I'm sure no one believed me. Everyone thought it was time for me to throw in the towel; everyone except God.

Donnie stayed a few minutes more before leaving for his day of making contacts and helping people. Our plan was to leave at 8 a.m. the next morning. He said he would come by and pick me up. I told him not to be late as it was a long drive. I also mentioned that Chad and Carma were meeting with us in their home on a Saturday and we didn't want to take up more time than needed by being late. As soon as he left, I called the attorney to postpone the appointment.

Knowing about the counseling seemed to help me relax a bit. I didn't think much about it, didn't want too, just wanted to have a stress-free day before a difficult counseling session the following day. I went to bed that night and for the first time in a while slept well.

I had my alarm set for 6:30, and at 5 a.m., Donnie came in to our bedroom. He had let himself in and decided he was going to crawl in bed with me. He reeked of alcohol and cigarette smoke. I was startled and instantly shaking. I asked him what he thought he was doing. He told me he was going to take a little nap before we left. I asked if he was just coming in and where he had been. This immediately irritated him. He angrily told me he had been with one of the young guys that he was "working" with. I left the bed in total disgust.

I woke Donnie at 7:00 so he would have time to shower. I had already explained to my girls why he was here, in my bed. They weren't happy about it, and it only confused Lexi. By the time I woke Donnie, I had already been online to check our bank account. Donnie had been at the casino all night. When I woke him, I confronted him about this and he was enraged. He told me he had taken a young man gambling all night. He had wanted to learn the blackjack tables, and it was a great way for them to spend time together. Donnie acted like I was the villain, how could I not see the good he had done? I asked him if he really felt he was helping these young jobless addicts by taking them to bars and casinos. Needless to say, by the time we left, Donnie was very angry at me. He explained he had given the kid money to gamble, money from our account. Then he told me how profusely the kid had thanked him when he took him home.

A few miles down the road, I shared a text Chad had sent me. It was a list of Bible verses that we needed to read to be ready for our session. I had brought the Bible along to do so. Donnie told me to read the verses while he drove. When I finished, that is when he started in on me.

For the next two hours straight, Donnie never stopped bashing me. He pointed out every fault I had, told me how all of our marriage problems were my fault. He told me I was a terrible mother, spoiling our girls and always putting them first. He bashed and blamed my mother and even my grandmother. He went on and on about how I was an anchor holding him down, how he would never choose me over God. He reminded me how God was behind all of his actions right now and I needed to get right with God so I could see this.

I was shaking so badly. I remember sitting so tense that my body hurt. I remember having my arms folded across my middle, kind of hugging myself, like all of my insides were about to fall out and I needed to hold them in. For two hours, this went on. He never stopped bashing, and when he ran out of things to say, he started over at the beginning.

I remember saying one thing. I asked him if he had anything that he needed to fix with Chad today. He told me no, that he was right with God and that he was closer to God than he had ever been. That was it. We were going to fix Lori today. In Donnie's eyes, that is what would save our marriage. That is why he had agreed to go.

Two hours with my body tense, shaking, barely breathing, I hadn't eaten, and I was crying. He just kept ranting at me. All of a sudden, we swerved left. I was confused. The ranting stopped and Donnie said he needed to get out of the truck and stretch. Then I saw it.

We were at a rest area. There, all over the parking lot were motorcycles. I remembered stopping here once before when the motorcycles had been here. The Christian Motorcycle Association was here passing out food, drink, and tracts. Donnie had seen it at the last minute and pulled in. He was excited! Before he even put it in park, I grabbed my phone and jumped from the truck. I started walking to a wooded area behind the rest stop. Donnie headed right for his fellow Christians. I figured he couldn't wait to tell them about his crazy wife. I was right.

When you are manic, you are loud. It didn't matter how far away I was, I could hear Donnie bashing me to the motorcyclist. He was asking them to pray for me, he told them we were going for counseling to save our marriage and again asked them to pray for me. I tuned him out. I knew what would come next: he would tell them how God was talking to him, leading him, and how I was holding him back. Then he would brag about Toby accepting Christ and all the "mission" work he was doing in our town. I had heard it a thousand times.

I leaned against a tree and looked at the little creek. I was shaking so badly I could hardly stand. I couldn't breathe. Why, God? Why would you let all of this happen to me again? I was furious with myself. This was my fault for even agreeing to come. I called Chad. I was crying hard by the time he answered. He asked where I was and if I was in danger. He asked if he needed to come pick me up. I told him I wasn't in physical danger, but I could not take this anymore. I couldn't go another hour or two in the car with Donnie. I told him what our ride had been like so far.

Chad threw out some scriptures, and I can't tell you what they were. They brought me no relief. Chad promised me that if I could get through the last part of the ride that he would not let what had happened on the ride go on during our session. I told him I felt like I had been held down and kicked in the stomach over and over. He told me I could do it, I could make it another few hours. He told me to pray, pray, pray, and continue to his house. Then he told me to come and expect to be free.

I stood a few minutes more. I didn't want to talk to the CMA people. I was sure they had believed Donnie's lies. I walked along the creek behind the rest stop. I could hear Donnie talking and laughing, telling everyone how great he was doing God's work. I could barely walk because of my shaking. I reached the pickup. Donnie always locked it but would leave the keys hidden on the truck. I checked every tire, every rim and ridge. He had taken the keys. I couldn't get in. I saw the CMA people looking at me. I paced back and forth beside the truck.

At one point, I stopped at the front of the truck. There in front of me was a four-lane highway. Traffic was moving fast. I counted semis passing. Then I had a plan. I knew that I could walk up to that four-lane, step out in front of a semi, and end all of my suffering. I began to shake even worse. I wanted to be done. I was too tired to do this anymore. Donnie had driven me to the point of insanity. I knew I was right with God and I knew where I would instantly be if I stepped out in front of one of those trucks. I would be in purple land, my land of comfort. I would instantly be in Jesus's arms. This nightmare would be over.

I leaned against the truck. I wanted to do it. It would happen so fast that there would be no pain. Then it hit me. There would be no pain for me, but what about my girls, my mom? How selfish was I being to put myself out of my misery but leave my girls to deal with this monster they called dad. What would happen to them? Donnie would have full control over Lexi, and I knew my three girls would not survive without me. I was so deep in thought, thinking this out, talking myself out of killing myself that I nearly had a heart attack when Donnie came up to me.

I looked at him, and I mean at him. He was there, Donnie himself, not the monster he had become, not the monster he had been for the last two hours. He told me there were some ladies who wanted to talk to me. I told him I had heard the lies he was telling them, that I was not going over there. If he hadn't been there, if I hadn't looked into his eyes and saw that it was him, we probably would have left. But it was him, the real Donnie, and I instantly felt sorry for him. I agreed to go talk to the ladies. Donnie tried to walk beside me and hold me up. I told him to get away from me. I could barely walk because I was shaking so badly. But I went, one foot in front of the other, like I had been doing for the last four months. One foot in front of the other, breathe, breathe.

CHAPTER 35

God Was There

The closer I got to the bikers, the more I shook. When I was probably a few yards away from them, four leather-clad women came to me and put their arms around me. They had encircled me, which pushed Donnie away from me. They quickly walked me away from him. I was shaking so hard that I could barely stand. I felt like I was having a full-blown seizure right there on my feet. I was crying hard and could not talk.

The women began to hug me and tell me they were praying for me. Nothing was mentioned about the lies I was sure Donnie had told them. I took a deep breath and told them to stop. I told them they didn't understand what was going on. I told them I was sure Donnie was bipolar and refused to get help and that he had been verbally bashing me for the last two hours. I told them we were on our way to counseling and that this was my last ditch effort to get him some help. One at a time, the four ladies told me that they understood. One by one, they told me the connection they had with me. One lady's first husband was bipolar. Another's stepfather was bipolar. The third had a bipolar brother, and the fourth also had a bipolar connection. I might not have all the connections right, but my point is, they had all been exposed to bipolar behavior and understood where I was at. They told me they had known right away that something was off with Donnie.

I knew then that my meeting them was no accident. God had brought us here; God had brought these women to me. I was so tired of people telling me God wouldn't give me more than I could handle. I no longer believed it. But with what was happening, I started to believe it again. I was in a pit, ready to end it all, and God brought me here, to these women who understood what was happening. I didn't have to try to convince them or explain anything to them. They all understood. They asked if they could pray for me. I was still surrounded and their arms were around me, and as they prayed, my shaking ceased. My body relaxed for the first time in several hours. They gave me some water and told me they would not stop praying. They gave me the courage to get back in that pick up and finish my journey.

That day, at a little rest area on the side of the road, I had hit rock bottom. I had considered ending my life to end the misery that surrounded me. Those CMA women saved my life. God saved my life. I had the courage to walk back to the truck and continue on. Donnie and I rode on in silence.

CHAPTER 36

Mohammed Taxi

We had been at the rest area for an hour. We were going to be late for sure. I told Donnie to call Chad and let him know we would be late. Because of this, I knew Donnie was totally aware of the time, but all of a sudden, he decided to stop again. He said he was thirsty and needed to get a drink now. He also said he was tired and needed me to drive the rest of the way. I knew he hadn't slept after being at the casino all night so that was fine with me.

I had calmed down considerably but was frustrated because we were late. Donnie took his time in the convenience store. When he came out, he had to pass in front of a taxi driver who was filling his cab with gas. I watched in the review mirror as Donnie stopped to chat. This was something that irritated me to no end. Just like on vacation, he had to stop and talk to everybody. Who cared if we were keeping Chad and Carma waiting? Donnie talked to the taxi driver for fifteen minutes while I sat and fumed. I saw them exchange numbers.

Donnie was very excited when he got in the truck. He had asked the guy about Jesus and the guy said he was going to call him later to visit. He told me his name was Mohammed. I didn't care. I just wanted to be out of the truck, be done being trapped in there with him. I drove with much rage. I knew by the GPS that we were getting close, and the closer we got, the nicer Donnie became. This enraged me further. I knew he was trying to butter me up so I wouldn't be upset when we got there, so I wouldn't tell Chad and Carma what had gone on during our ride.

When we were about one block away from their house, we passed a convenience store that was named Holiday. Donnie shared that he felt this was a sign and began to reminisce with me about his favorite holidays we had spent together. This made me even angrier. How dare he decide to be nice to me and bring up happy memories now after the bashing he had done earlier?

We arrived and got out. Chad was outside and went to hug Donnie. As soon as I stepped out, I began to cry and shake again. We went inside. While Donnie took a bathroom break, I told Chad and Carma that he had been out gambling all night. They already knew about the ride since I had called them. Donnie came out all chipper. I'm sure he was excited to finally get his wife fixed! Then we began the longest counseling session in history.

CHAPTER 37

Hope

I will do my best to explain what happened that day, but I will keep it brief. I do not feel I can rightfully explain the work Chad and Carma do. I will tell you it involves cleansing yourself, getting rid of demons and bad things that have taken up residence in your body and mind. I have mentioned before that we do a lot of alternative medicine with our daughter Kaylee. When I try to explain that to people, they really can't understand it until they have witnessed it or experienced it themselves. That is what I would compare our counseling session too. If someone were to sit and tell me about it, I would have trouble wrapping my head around it.

Chad told me to sit by Carma and he had Donnie sit across the room. I liked this immediately. I didn't want to be near him. Chad told me that Carma had been doing some research on some massage therapy and she began to rub my back and shoulders. I began to relax and my shaking stopped. Next thing you know, I was sitting on the floor in front of Carma, feeling more relaxed than I had in months.

Chad explained to us what would be happening and told us it was time to get started. He asked who wanted to go first. I told him, very sarcastically, that I would start because I was apparently the one with all the problems. He had me close my eyes. Chad asked me my name then. Who are you? The more he talked, the more Carma rubbed my knots, the more relaxed I became. I didn't quite understand the concept of what was taking place. He asked me who I was again and I told him: Lori.

He had me open my eyes and then explained to me where we were going with this. For example, when he asked my name, he was actually calling to something that had taken up dwelling in my body, mind, and soul. I might answer something like, doubt, and then Chad would begin praying out the doubt, kicking it out, telling it to leave. As doubt, brought in by Satan, left, I would begin to fill up the empty places he left with God. That is the best I can do to explain it, I know I'm not doing it justice.

Chad had me close my eyes again, then asked me who I was. Again, nothing came to me and I said, Lori. He had me open my eyes again and asked me what I was seeing with my eyes closed. I smiled for the first time that day and explained I was seeing purple. He asked me if purple represented something to me and I told him what I had learned at the The Living Center counseling sessions. I told him I was so relaxed I felt like a wet noodle and couldn't get up if he asked me too.

That is when we moved on to Donnie. Again, I feel this is not really my story to tell. I will tell you that Donnie got rid of a lot of junk, stuff from his childhood, stuff he had brought in with his new infatuation of Native American ancestors; he got rid of things that I never knew about. It took several hours and it was emotional and exhausting for him.

I will share some things that pertain to me. Donnie admitted he had a gambling problem. He visited with Chad about the bars and dance clubs. We talked about the other women Donnie had desired to pursue, about his hyper behavior. Finally, everything that had been upsetting to me was on the table.

I had shared that we had an upcoming psychiatry appointment. Carma told me then that it was good we had counseling before. She said if they would have given Donnie medication, then the session probably wouldn't have gone so well. She explained that the medicine could have kept Donnie from opening up to his past and getting rid of the things he had. Carma also shared a tool with me for dealing with Donnie when he was lecturing, preaching, ranting, and raving. I could hardly wait to share it with my girls. They tried it and so did I and it really worked. When Donnie would start in, under my breath, I would pray, "God, please shut his mouth now." This technique was used very frequently in our home after that.

Hours later, when we left, I felt like we had made great progress. I remember at one point Chad looking at Donnie and telling him this, "Donnie, your energy and excitement are so awesome." Then he said, "Your energy and excitement exhaust me." Amen to that. Through our session, Donnie admitted he was wrong to be out dancing, and he promised to give up the bars and gambling. By the time we left, I could see Donnie again. I felt he had been healed. He was so…himself.

We left and it was late. We found the nearest hotel exhausted. The next day, we started our journey home. Donnie was excited for the progress he had made. He made several phone calls on the way home to let people know how things had gone. The ride home was pleasant. Donnie was kind. It is like he had been totally set free of everything that had tortured us for the last four months. I had hope. I was anxious to get home and tell our girls.

CHAPTER 38

There They Are Again

The next day, we headed home. I noticed huge changes, positive changes. I did notice that some of the racing thoughts were still there and Donnie still seemed obsessed with saving the world. When we stopped for gas, Donnie still insisted on talking to everyone. This time, it was a guy on a motorcycle. Donnie visited with him about his bike and the kid told him of an accident he had had. Donnie told him that someone must have been watching out for him. Donnie told him about the CMA people at the rest area.

This incident is worth mentioning for two reasons. One, Donnie tried his best to keep it brief, which was a change.

And I tried my best to show some patience. This was also a change. More importantly, we would meet with this young man again, just down the road.

As we got near the rest area, the one from the day before, Donnie asked if the CMA people were still there if we should stop. I agreed we should. When we pulled in, there was the young kid we had just met an hour before. His bike was parked and one of the CMA bikers was off talking to him about Jesus. This touched my heart and I knew that God was using Donnie, even in his manic behaviors to reach out to people.

We crossed the parking lot and all eyes were on us. I'm sure our behaviors from the day before were still in their minds. We were greeted with hugs. My "ladies" instantly came to me. I told them things had gone well and thanked them again for their help. One lady told me that she lived twenty miles from me and gave me her card. I promised to keep in touch.

Before we left, my new friend told me that she and several of the ladies there that day had decided that it was more important to pray than sleep. They had stayed up through the night to pray for us. And they had contacted more CMA people and the need for prayer was passed nationwide through the biking association. She told me that there had literally been thousands of people praying for us the night before. I was speechless and the tears came. I can't tell you how much I needed to hear this. It was the boost in my faith that I needed at that time.

We headed home. Donnie said he needed to continue living across the street. He felt he needed the time alone to dig into his Bible and spend time with God. He also said he felt he needed to prove himself, that he could stay out of the bars before I let him back in. I was all in favor of that. But by the end of the trip, we had decided we were ready to live as a family again and he would move home right away.

I had called the girls the night before to let them know the counseling session had gone well. They were anxious for details. When we arrived home, Donnie called a family meeting. We explained what had taken place and the changes that we had both already seen. Donnie promised them no more bars or casinos. He asked if he could go back to the bar one more time to tell his new friends to keep in touch and that he would love to see them, but it would have to be away from the bar. He said it would be in and out, no drinking. Our girls and I agreed that this was fair. I don't think Donnie ever made that visit.

Things continued to improve. Donnie was home each night. However, he didn't go to bed at a normal time. To him, home meant in the driveway or in view of the house. If he couldn't go to the bars, then he would stay outside in the garage or visit with the neighbors who stayed up till all hours of the night. I could see a pull there. He was staying at home because he said he would. It wasn't where he wanted to be. He was drawn to the bars and had to fight it. I asked him and he admitted this was true.

CHAPTER 39

Psych Appointment

The psychiatry appointment I had made months ago was finally here. Donnie had improved greatly. He was willing to go, he said, to give me peace. He was better, but I was still seeing some manic behaviors. We headed that direction. Donnie didn't seem too stressed about it. I was stressed. I wanted a diagnosis so that things would get all the way back to normal. On our drive there, Donnie seemed pretty calm, and in my heart, I knew we would not get a diagnosis that day.

The psychiatrist started with sharing the notes from the psychologist we had seen. He said that the psychologist had suggested bipolar to us and said that Donnie displayed many symptoms. That is why he had made the recommendation to us to visit with this new guy.

The doctor looked at Donnie and asked him what had been going on. Donnie explained and added the newest information from our counseling session. He told the doctor that he believed he was being spiritually attacked and at the same time he was trying new things and pursuing ministry.

I listened and with each sentence my heart sank. The doctor looked at me and I briefly explained, like I always did, about four years ago and how it was repeating itself. I told him I believed he was bipolar. The doctor looked at me and said, "You have done your research and you know that I cannot give him a bipolar diagnosis today, don't you?" I said yes. He went on to explain that if Donnie was bipolar, he couldn't just turn off the manic behavior today for his visit. I told him the manic had been lessening, but yes, I knew what research said. I told the doctor I had watched him turn it off and on for months now. When he was around certain people or certain situations, he could act totally normal. I knew in my heart that that didn't fit the bipolar description.

I began to cry. I had waited months for this appointment. Yes, Donnie had been better, but he was still having manic behavior, still wasn't working on a regular basis. That is when I told the doctor I couldn't keep doing this. I told him one of us was leaving there that day with medication. If he wasn't going to prescribe any for Donnie, then I needed something for anxiety. He agreed and wrote me a prescription.

When the doctor saw how upset I was, he said that he thought Donnie was having a midlife crisis. Later, when I researched, the signs and symptoms of a midlife crisis are very similar to bipolar manic behavior. Donnie was thrilled with this information. The thought of being bipolar was humiliating, but having a midlife crisis seemed very intriguing to him. He was quick to tell people about this, almost bragging about it, like it somehow made him younger, cooler.

Donnie felt he had held up his end of the bargain. He had gone to the appointment, and now he had proof in his mind, he was fine and I was the one with the problem. Even without meds, Donnie continued to improve. I didn't have to use the anxiety medication very often.

During the day, Donnie continued to reach out to people. He continued to pursue starting a business or two. He continued to help everyone while things at our house fell apart. I kept up best I could, but there were just some things I needed help with. His hoarding continued, and I had piles of junk everywhere, inside and out.

I tried not to complain. Staying out of the bars was huge. Yet he wasn't back all the way. I was just as lonely as I was before, even with him living at home. He was never here. He told me every place he was going and checked in with me often. He always asked me to go along. I had no desire. I called Carma to visit and she agreed that she felt Donnie needed to come back for another session. I scheduled one and Donnie agreed to go as long as we were back in time for him to follow through with his plans. He had scheduled a cage fight. He and a few other guys were going. Donnie hadn't told me right away. For me, this was just another sign that things still weren't right.

He agreed to go to counseling, but we had to be finished by a certain time, in order for him to get back in time to leave for his fight. This frustrated me. What could be more important than our counseling session? Not a cage fight! He begged me to go watch. He wanted me to bring Lexi to watch. I told him no. Quite honestly, Lexi is a fan of cage fighting. She likes to watch it on TV. I asked her if she was disappointed that she couldn't go watch her dad. She told me no and said that her dad wasn't ready. He hadn't trained enough and he had never done it before. She didn't think the outcome would be good and she didn't want to go. I had to agree. Many people had advised Donnie that age forty-three was not a time to start cage fighting, that is the time most people got out of it. Donnie said he was going to make lots of money at it. He also mentioned that maybe someday, there would be a movie about him and how he started his cage fighting career at a late age and became a legend. Yes, we needed to go back for more counseling.

The counseling session was to take place very early on a Saturday morning so Donnie could get back. We had to leave the night before or get up in the middle of the night to leave. Since I had Donnie sleeping more, I decided it would be best to go the night before. The drive for the second counseling session was much better than the first. We were headed in the right direction; there were just a few more bumps in the road.

Donnie got frequent calls from Mohammed Taxi. God had definitely brought that connection about. He called while we were traveling that day. I liked Mohammed instantly when Donnie put the call on speaker. He had asked why we were heading back in that direction. Donnie had told him we were going to counseling. Mohammed asked why. Donnie told him he hadn't been treating his wife the way he should. For the next five minutes, I listened to Mohammed lecture Donnie about treating his wife well and how he should always do that and be ashamed of himself if he didn't. Yes, Mohammed was a good guy in my book!

CHAPTER 40

Session Two

Session 2 was not quite as intense as the first one. I was happy to share the positive improvements I had seen in Donnie and he did the same. I had some things I felt I could visit with Chad and Carma about this time. I was more than ready to get rid of the distrust I had had for Donnie and even for God. I also wanted to get rid of the anger and doubt.

We started with Donnie. He was able to talk through some more things and get rid of some more junk. I was happy about this. Chad talked to him about the cage fight. Donnie told him it was only about competition. He loved to compete and he had always wanted to do this. I wasn't so sure. Donnie wanted to hold on to that even though Chad and Carma advised against it. He also refused to give up the smoking he had started. He told Chad he liked it and could quit when he wanted, but he didn't want too at this time.

I shared with Chad that I was still seeing some manic behavior in Donnie. I talked about Donnie not working, about his pull to leave the house at night even though he hadn't. I told him that Donnie's desire to help people was almost like an addiction. Chad told me that God had brought that to his mind already. He talked to Donnie then about trying to force me into getting involved with all the people Donnie was involved with. I had told Chad that I was tired of women calling and knocking on the door because they wanted to see Donnie, always needing his help, always needing a hug from him. Chad addressed this as well, telling Donnie his ministry should be with men and that he needed to find someone to get involved with the ladies, since my plate was full at this time. He also talked to him about putting some limits on his helping people. Chad asked Donnie to really pray about things and for him and me to pray about them together before acting. He reminded Donnie that he couldn't do it all, he had to say no sometimes. It was a good session.

The thing that stuck out to me most during this visit was when Chad and Carma asked me to join them by putting my hands on Donnie's head. They then prayed for healing for anything that might be wrong in his head, anything that was there that shouldn't be.

By the time it was my turn, it was time to leave. Donnie couldn't be late for the big fight. I felt most of what was hindering to me was caused by Donnie's manic behaviors, so I hoped that in time, all that was troubling me would disappear. We headed home, and again, the drive was peaceful. We both felt we had made progress. I was ready for a night of relaxation while Donnie was ready to head to his fight. He was very excited.

CHAPTER 41

The Fight

Two days after we laid our hands on Donnie's head and prayed for healing, I saw more drastic changes. Donnie will also tell you that two days after it happened, he felt different, better. But not before his big fight.

He kept me posted. I, along with everybody in his contact list, received a picture of him after his first fight. His eye was badly swollen. Donnie had called me. I received the picture first and was upset. He said he had received a knee to his temple. He said the referee told him if he got hit again, it would break open so they called the fight. Donnie told me he was going to forfeit his next match. He said the blow to his head had made him realize that his family was more important than some cage fight.

Later, he called to tell me he had decided to fight in the next match. His opponent had agreed to a fight using submission holds only, no hitting. Donnie won this fight. He got a medal and a chance to talk in the microphone. He was proud to tell me that he had bragged about his love for me and then given all the glory to God. In his eyes, this justified his fight. It did nothing but sicken me.

It would be a few hours before Donnie got home. During this time, I felt a depression-like mood come over me. I just wanted to go to bed and sleep. I was in bed when Donnie came home. He had expected me to be up and greeting him. I was not interested one bit in seeing his badly swollen face.

The next morning was Sunday. I will do my best to explain to you what happened to me that day. When I woke, I felt unable to get out of bed. The best way for me to describe it is that it felt as if I had cement in my veins. My body felt heavy and I was very tired. I was unable to get out of bed to go to church. Maybe part of it was not wanting to face my church family and listen to everyone ask about Donnie's face and then stand there and listen while he explained it. I'm not sure what it was, but it would happen again, several times.

Each time this did happen to me, it was a Sunday. Most of the time, Donnie was patient and would leave church and check on me. He would try to lovingly coax me to go and was understanding when I couldn't. But after it had happened several times, his patience wore thin. The last time it happened, I remember him coming in, ripping the covers off me and telling me to get up, that my girls needed me. I began to cry and told him if anyone should understand, it should be him. I had been patient with him for months when he was depressed.

The better things got with Donnie, the fewer episodes I had with this experience. It only happened on Sundays. Each time, Satan would fill my head with things. Things like mental images of Donnie hugging young women at church. I often got the mental image that I had seen over and over in real life, Donnie holding other people's children at church while Lexi sat and watched with sad eyes. I believe all of this was a spiritual battle. Each time, the episode would be totally gone by Monday morning.

Things were getting better. Each day, I saw less and less manic behavior. Donnie continued to run a small handyman business. He also took a lineman job an hour away. I knew he did this to shut me up and try to bring me peace. Because of this job, he was unable to complete the jobs he had already agreed to for his handyman business. The person he was so intent on helping could not be counted on to show up. So I became the handyman. I wanted him to keep working so I felt forced into completing these jobs. Donnie acted like he expected me to do it.

I will tell you, I am no handyman. I have learned to do much on my own with Donnie working on the road. But I was being asked to complete tasks I had no idea how to do, things I was scared to do. I am afraid of heights, and one day, I found myself on a ladder on a roof working. It terrified me, but it had to be done.

Very quickly, the handyman jobs became mine. I had already taken on one of the jobs I had lined up when Donnie told me I had better find work to support myself. Donnie did not like this now. He told me I was not trusting God to provide if I felt I had to take a job. I told him often that God had provided by giving me the job. I did not feel God was going to go make a deposit in our bank account, especially when he wasn't really looking to work. This was still a sore subject between us.

Finally, I told Donnie I couldn't do it anymore. All the people he started the business for, all the people he wanted to help, were not reliable workers. I did not feel they could be unsupervised and trusted. He agreed. A lot of times, they didn't even show up. I was tired and the jobs were too hard for me. Slowly, he started to let this business go. He had basically made no money on it so far, so it was a clean loss.

Donnie complained often about no longer wanting to be a lineman, about not being content in what he was doing. One thing Donnie did like about his job an hour away was the opportunities it gave him to pick up hitchhikers. I was against this. I still am against this. I don't feel it is safe this day in age. However, there was one man that I must tell you about.

Donnie picked up Michael and immediately called me. He knew he wasn't supposed to bring the hitchhikers to our house, but he wanted permission. Michael was a Christian and he needed a few things. He had nothing, his wallet and belongings had all been stolen. He had been walking in the heat for days, sleeping in ditches. When I met Michael, my heart melted.

He was a military vet and was also disabled. He worked where he could. At the time Donnie picked him up, he was traveling to St. Louis. His story was a sad one. One night, many years ago, Michael was in a bar having a few drinks with friends. He decided not to drive home, so called his wife to come get him. She had to bring their young son along, and on their way to the bar, mother and son were killed in an accident. Michael said he would never drive again after his family was killed. He also blamed himself. Michael was on his way to visit their grave. While there, he would replace all of his legal papers that were stolen with his wallet.

Michael immediately reminded me of Donnie's stepdad, Ike. I liked him instantly. Lexi made his face light up, and we gave him a few necessities and set him up to sleep at our church. The next day, our pastor would take him to the bus and he would leave. Our church provided the bus ticket. I took Lexi to tell him good-bye before school that day. I made sure he had our contact information and some food and money for his trip.

I asked Michael to stay. He said he had to visit the grave sites. He promised to return. We never heard from Michael again. Maybe someday, we will. Sometimes, I wonder if this was a test. Donnie was doing God's work. I had become judgmental. Michael was just a man down on his luck and Donnie was willing to help him. Michael melted my heart and I began to feel again. I had spent the last several months making my heart so hard so I would feel nothing. Michael gave me hope that maybe someday, my heart would heal.

CHAPTER 42

Diagnosis

The manic behavior was finally gone, all of it. If you asked me, I would say that Donnie was doing well. I would tell you he had been healed. I do believe that the counseling we did helped him out of his manic behavior. It helped him to come to terms with a lot of junk in his life. But after a few weeks of manic-free behavior, I started to see depression.

At first, Donnie blamed this on one young man he had been dedicated to helping. Donnie finally figured out what I had been telling him was true. The kid was using him, abusing Donnie's acts of kindness toward him. The young man was soon picked up with a DWI, and shortly after we heard, he was pretty heavy into drugs again. Donnie asked me one day if I thought this was what was causing his depression. I told him no. I told him I believed he was bipolar and could we please get some help. He asked me to be patient. He wanted to try to work through the depression. I was patient for two weeks. Throughout that time, I asked him more than once if he still believed that I had caused his depression four years ago. He told me that he did not believe that.

When he was home from work, he sat and watched TV or stayed in bed. He slept a lot. My patience was wearing thin. Just when I thought I couldn't take it anymore, Donnie asked me to call and make an appointment with the psychiatrist. It would be two weeks before we could get in. When Donnie heard this, he asked me to make an appointment that day with a medical doctor to get him something to help him over the hump until the upcoming appointment.

That day, the doctor gave him an antidepressant after Donnie's explanation of what had been happening the last several months. Then the doctor told him he thought Donnie was probably bipolar. He encouraged us to keep the psychiatric appointment.

I didn't notice any change with the medication but continued to be patient. I knew these things sometimes took up to two weeks to start working. I was anxious for the psych appointment. Would we finally get a diagnosis?

Appointment day came and Donnie explained what had been happening. Then Donnie looked at the doctor and said,

"Am I bipolar?" The doctor said yes, that he was definitely in a cycle of bipolar manic and depression. For the next half hour, I asked questions and listened. I learned a lot that day. I was confused as this is the same doctor who would not give a diagnosis before. I guessed that maybe because the depression was hitting, he was convinced of the cycle.

The doctor told us about many famous people who are bipolar: Robin Williams and Patty Duke to name a few. He told us bipolar is the same thing as manic depressive, just a name change in 1985. He talked to us about medications. Lithium would be used to control the manic behavior. Donnie could still have episodes, but the medication would cause them to be less severe and farther apart. He also told me that just because it was four years between episodes doesn't mean that is the cycle he would stay on. He could have another episode next week. This made me shiver.

The doctor also told us that most people that are bipolar have their first episode in their thirties or fifties. Donnie was in his early forties. He explained there are no rules. He then told us if we were lucky, Donnie might not have any more manic episodes. If he did, the doctor warned us that it would be very difficult to keep him on medication. When you are manic, you feel great, everything is good in your world. You don't think you need the medication. This would be the greatest challenge.

There you have it. After six and a half months, I got the diagnosis I was looking for. Donnie spent the next few hours pretty quiet and with tears in his eyes. A bipolar diagnosis is not an easy thing to swallow. I felt we had rounded a corner, overcome the odds; I felt like I had just woke up from a terrible nightmare, a nightmare that had lasted six months.

CHAPTER 43

Back to Life

Today, Donnie is very faithful about taking his medication. I ask him daily and sometimes twice a day if he has taken it. The other day, I asked him if he was tired of me questioning him about his meds every day. He said no and told me I had a right to. I know that he wants to take them, he wants to be better. He still struggles with the diagnosis. He feels there is a stigma attached to it. Since the diagnosis it seems to me that so many commercials and television shows, books, talk shows, etc., are about bipolar disorder. To me, it seems it is becoming more commonly diagnosed. Or maybe I just wasn't paying attention before.

Donnie is able to work and focus. Does he love his lineman work? It depends on the day. Most of the time, he says it is a good job and he certainly doesn't hate it. We continue to plug away at our debt that acquired over the last six months. Donnie continued his job an hour away.

God brings us through it one day at a time. Just like four years ago, it is hard to face some people. Donnie doesn't always remember what he said or how he acted in front of them. Some of the things he does remember make it hard to face certain people. Most people are kind and forgiving.

Donnie's desires that became intense during his manic phase are all gone. The small business is done. I don't believe that Donnie is a gambling addict, unless he is manic. He is not even tempted by it. The drinking and wandering are done. The desire to cage fight is gone. The smoking is done. Those are all things that are only important to him during his manic phase, and once that was gone, he quit these things without struggle.

I have learned a lot. I try not to nag. Once I quit nagging about the smoking and cage fighting, they just went away. It took over two months for the sores on my head to go away, just like four years ago. During Donnie's manic phase, I was so stressed I couldn't eat. Now that life is better, I have gained forty pounds, just like four years ago. This is frustrating; unfortunately, I am a stress eater, and even though things are better, there is still a lot of stress.

I have removed myself from anything that takes any energy on my part. Relay is done for me. It will always be near and dear to my heart, but it is a constant reminder to me of my dad's death, my kids' illnesses, and Donnie's manic episodes. It is a constant reminder of really horrible times in my life. It doesn't seem like I am supposed to help with that ministry any more.

I also removed myself from everything at church. No more children's ministry, no more nursery work, no more helping with anything. This is just the way it is right now. Go, hear a sermon and music, and go home. I talk to the people around me and the ones I pass coming and going from my seat. I remember the days when I was one of the first people up to meet a visitor. Now I can't tell you the names of many of the new people in our church.

For six months, I not only trained my heart to be hard and feel nothing, but I put up walls, high walls. I avoided going anywhere, I avoided people. I didn't want questions, and I didn't want to hear other people's problems. I have noticed now, as I am healing, that this is still a struggle. I find myself feeling awkward around people.

And some people that did know what was going on, people who were very involved at the time, say nothing now. Do they just think everything went away, that no healing needs to take place? Do they not think that we still need to hear the words, "We are praying for you"? I understand that people might not know what to say. To me, this reminds me of when someone loses a loved one. People rally around them, but soon, they are on their own. Now I know they must feel forgotten. It is hurtful for people not to ask, not to just say, "Hey, we are still praying for you, how are things going." This makes me feel hurt and angry. It especially angers me when people know Donnie is at times back on the road, alone, and no one reaches out to him. Do people not understand he has an illness and wasn't in control of his actions? It is frustrating and just reassures me that healing and forgiveness still need to take place. It is a slow process.

Trust has become a problem for me that was never there before. I find myself snooping in Donnie's phone, checking his contacts and messages. He assures me all of that behavior is gone, and my snooping proves to me I have nothing to worry about. How does one learn to trust again? When you trust with your whole heart, like I did, only to find out maybe you shouldn't be, it is hard to recover from that. I hate not trusting fully. I know Donnie's behavior that caused the mistrust is bipolar/manic behavior. In my heart, I know I have nothing to worry about. Healing, it is a process.

It has taken all of my energy and focus to get past this ordeal. Maybe someday I can go back to all of those things that I loved dearly. I know some people probably think I am rude, they probably remember that I used to be friendly and outgoing. Maybe they remember how I used to send them cards or just stop to chat. Those days are gone for now. Right now, my focus is on healing myself and my family.

It really was like a reoccurring nightmare, only this time much, much worse. My heart is still hard at times. I'm working on it, but these days, I have little sympathy for the person complaining to me about their husband being gone for three days. I have little sympathy for the person telling me about all their ailments and how awful they feel. I trained my heart for six months to feel nothing. I trained it well. Once in a while, something will get to me and I know that I'm headed in the right direction to a loving heart again.

A hard heart was my coping mechanism. Now I know that the only coping mechanism I needed was Jesus Christ. He was with me every step. When I felt alone and full of panic, it was because I was not turning things over to God. I was trying to handle things from a human perspective. There was nothing anyone could do. My only hope was God. All the times I temporarily went crazy, I had taken my focus off God. God is the one who reminded me to put one foot in front of the other and breathe.

Our girls have recovered well. Once in a while, Lexi will ask questions. I answer them honestly. The other day, she asked me, in her nine-year-old way, "Mom, what will we do if Daddy goes psychic again?" Psychic isn't the word I would use to describe it, but I understood what she meant. The only answer I had for her is, "We will pray our way through it, Lexi."

The anger and stress caused by their dad is not forgotten, but it is forgiven. The other day, Kaylee had a friend come up to her and say something about her dad's behavior in the weight room. Kaylee knew from what he was saying that he had seen Donnie at the top of his manic phase. Smile and move on. That is all you can do. Kaylee recently woke from a nightmare, shaking and teary. In the night terror, he was manic again, preaching at her, not being kind.

I know that Satan uses Donnie's illness against us. He uses it to cause doubt in both of us. There are times that Satan creeps into my thoughts, and I wonder if Donnie is thinking about the other woman, the one he loved for a day.

The other day, some friends of ours were asking Donnie a few questions. They said something about him feeling better now than when he was manic. He had to disagree. He said, "You feel great when you are manic. That is the problem."

I often have people that already know my story come up to me and say how much they admire me, how strong I am, some have even called me a hero. None of this is true. I could not have gotten through any of this without Jesus Christ, my savior. He was with me every step. He gave me strength, He guided me. Every time I wanted to walk away, He had me stay. And look where it got me. I love Donnie now more than I ever have. I can't even remember when the last time is that we even had a slight disagreement. We have more respect for each other.

It is hard not to play the what-if game. What if I would have filed for divorce when Donnie asked me too? What if Donnie had taken his day of being in love with another woman one step farther? What if I had stepped out in front of one of those semis? What if? There is no reason to play that game. God is and was in control the whole time. God protected me and our girls. God protected Donnie, kept him safe all those times he drove without sleep.

Four years ago, I started this book. Then I set it aside. Once things happened again, and when it finally came to an end, I knew I did not have the strength to write it all down. I hadn't planned on a part 2. I sat in church for two months straight, hearing none of the sermon. I was in a constant argument each Sunday with God. He kept prodding me to write it down. I didn't want to. God would and still does wake me in the night with something I need to add, something I had forgotten that he wants on the pages.

I am convinced that even if I help one person, it would be worth reliving all of it. It has been a difficult journey. Each day, I would type for one hour. That was all I could handle, and it usually ended in an episode of hives. So many times, I wanted to stop. God kept pushing me to do it. It was brought to my mind not too long ago, something my dad said in his last days: "I have waited my whole life to do the things I wanted to do, and now it is too late." I knew I couldn't wait.

So I did it. I know that this is a hard thing for my husband. And I have to live with the fear that having others read this could be enough to push Donnie into a manic episode. Still, God is pushing. Donnie told me he would read it when I was done. Now that it is done, he says he isn't ready to read it but to move forward with it.

Through everything that happened, I believe Donnie is the real hero. He has admitted to having a medical condition that to him is humiliating. He has faced people after they saw him at his worst. He is brave and courageous. Donnie's love and compassion for people magnified during his manic phase. It controlled him and he took it overboard. That was the illness, not Donnie. Donnie's heart has always been in the right place.

I know also that some people won't be happy when they read it; relationships could be forever severed. I will tell you that I have not typed anything that wasn't true, I typed it the way I saw it, the way I lived it. I am sorry if it is hurtful to some. That isn't my intention. Everyone makes mistakes and no one knew what to do to help. People have been forgiven and I hope I will be too. There are still many hurts that need mended after so many cries for help. The saddest thing about betrayal is that it never comes from your enemies. It comes from friends and loved ones. I've learned that forgiveness is forgiveness, but it doesn't mean letting someone hurt you over and over. Forgiveness sets you free. The other people are still responsible for making changes.

And now the book is done, the hard part anyway. I believe God used bipolar to grow Donnie and I, spiritually, as husband and wife, as parents, as Christians. Before Donnie got sick, I was stagnant in my faith. I feel my growing season began with the bipolar disease; however, there were many things along the way that were a part of it. I know Julio was put in my life to change my attitude toward people. It did.

Even though he has caused me much heartache and still at times continues to make bad choices, I will always love that young man with all my heart.

The unexplained illness of Taylor brought her to live at home for when I would need her here the most. Kaylee's health issues over the years—all part of our growing pains. My girls are strong because of what they have endured, and more importantly, all three of them have Jesus living in their hearts.

During Donnie's manic phase, I felt I hit rock bottom. I am ashamed of the way I acted at times, the words that came out of my mouth, the hatred that spewed out of me. At times, I literally felt I had gone crazy with no hope of return. The times I doubted God, yelled at God, questioned God, were all part of my growing season. I am thankful that I am loved by a forgiving God. I have come to realize the past is in the past and I need to let it go. This is easier said than done.

I have learned that growing seasons don't end. Not when God is involved. I will continue to grow, be pruned, fertilized, shined on, and rained on, until that final harvest. God had some important lessons for me to learn over the last four years and even more for the rest of my life. I will never understand why it had to happen, why it happened twice. And I pray with my every fiber that there will not be a part 3 to this book.

Recently, I attended a wedding. Pat came up to me after the ceremony. She is the lady who told me to follow my heart and not my head, because God works in your heart. She put her arm around me and said, "We have no idea what for better or worse means when we say those vows do we?" She is so right. I took my vows seriously twenty-five years ago, but I realize I was only repeating the words, not really thinking them through. I'm not naive enough to think that things couldn't be even worse than they were. But I could never have imagined surviving what we did. God would not let me walk away. So many times I wanted to, so many times I did. God kept bringing me back, sometimes kicking and screaming. Now I feel I understand what for better or worse means. No matter how awful it was, I would do it again. Donnie is the love of my life.

I feel that one of the most important lessons on what we have gone through, four years ago, and now, is that God works, even in the most stressful situations. Between the two times that Donnie was manic, I know of at least three people who gave their lives to Christ, and I know of one homeless man that Donnie talked out of suicide, right in my living room. Yes, God was working and those awesome things make it worth the suffering that occurred.

I think my growing season probably has something to do with fully relying on God like I never had before. I am a believer that everything happens for a reason and I believe that someday soon, God will show Donnie and me why. Until then, I continue to reach toward the Son!

The following information is from pamphlets we got from the psychiatrist when Donnie was diagnosed: Bipolar Disorder by GlaxoSmithKline and Living with Bipolar Disorder by Eli Lilly and Company.

What is bipolar disorder?

* Bipolar affects about 2 million Americans (3 out of every 100 adults). It does not discriminate between age, race, gender, ethnicity, education, or occupation. Not everyone's symptoms are the same and there is no blood test to confirm a diagnosis. Bipolar is an illness that deals with two extremes, mania and depression. It does tend to run in families, but genetic inheritance is not always the case. Bipolar disorder frequently runs in families when more than one family member suffers from bipolar disorder or depression. If there is a history of bipolar disorder or depression in your family, you have a higher risk of developing a mood disorder.
* Symptoms of mania include: intense moods, increased energy, wild and reckless behavior, little need for sleep. You may feel that you never want these symptoms to end.
* Symptoms of depression include: sadness, hopelessness, exhaustion.

* Some people experience a cycle of these moods. Those who do not have a cycling pattern can be affected by outside events, personal problems, change of seasons, etc.
* How often and how strong these moods are depends on each person.

Types of bipolar disorder:

* Bipolar I Disorder: requires at least one episode of manic or mixed episode in a lifetime
* Bipolar II Disorder: requires only one episode of a hypomanic episode plus one major depressive episode in a person's lifetime

Different kinds of mood episodes associated with bipolar disorder:

* Mania: high energy, creativity, social ease, little need for sleep, racing thoughts, trouble focusing, more talkative than usual and talking loudly, more self-confident than usual, focused on getting things done but completing little, risky and unusual activities to the extreme: these can progress to extreme highs, agitation, irritability, and for some violence.

    You might feel invincible, almost superhuman. A manic episode can also lead to hallucinations or delusions. A manic episode can last a week or more.

* Hypomania: Most of the symptoms of this are the same as mania but milder. You might feel better than usual and get more done. This can last at least four days.

* Depression: feeling sad, loss of interest in things you normally enjoy, feeling worthless, guilty, hopeless, sleeping too little or too much, change in weight and appetite, feeling tired and having little energy, feeling restless, problems concentrating and making decisions, thoughts of death and suicide. This can last for two weeks or more.

* Mixed episodes: blend of mania and depression, they can occur at the same time or cycle throughout the day. This lasts at least a week.

* Risky behaviors associated with bipolar disorder: Agitation, irritability, violence, excessive gambling, argumentative, mounting debt, legal/criminal issues, risky sex or change in sexual pattern, talking about hurting oneself, impulsive financial investments, relationship problems, poor decision making, careless spending or buying sprees, change in energy level, appetite, or sleep, abuse of alcohol and drugs.

* Cycling: The number of cycles that occur varies from person to person.

* Having four or more cycles in a year is called rapid cycling.

* Cycles don't always alternate between highs and lows. You could have three depressive episodes followed by one manic episode or vice versa.

Medication

* Medicines that suppress swings between mania or depression: these delay or relieve episodes of mania or depression. Regular blood tests to check your levels are sometimes required with these.
* Medicines that treat depression: these are often combined with the above medications.
* Taking your medicine: Some medications start working right away, others take a few days or weeks before they have an effect. It is important not to miss a dose of medicine to keep the levels of medication steady in your body. When you are having a manic episode, it is difficult for a person to stay on their medication because they feel good and don't feel that they need it.
* Just like any other illness, if bipolar is not treated properly episodes may become more frequent and severe.

Triggers: Not having regular sleep patterns, using illegal drugs and alcohol, stopping your medications, using herbal products, seasonal changes, holidays, illness, disagreements with family and friends, problems at work, death of a loved one.

Other: Keeping your bipolar illness a secret is not a good idea. It will help to have family, friends, and work understand what you are going through. It is an illness and nothing to be ashamed of. Counseling can be very helpful.

Helping a friend or family member with bipolar disorder:

The chances are good that you will feel helpless to do anything to help. The chances are also good that, as a family member, you are probably one of the people most deeply affected and hurt by your loved one's bipolar disorder.

What can you do to help someone who is bipolar

* Educate yourself on bipolar disorder.
* Realize that bipolar disorder is real and treatable. It isn't a weakness or character flaw; it is related to a chemistry problem in the brain.
* Realize it is not their fault and it's not your fault.
* Realize you can't fix the illness.
* You need to be caring, understanding, and supportive, and patient.
* Never give up hope.
* Help the person with bipolar disorder stay on their medications.
* Encourage them to get professional help/counseling.
* Recognize the symptoms early on.

* Help develop a plan to handle episodes. Do this when they are stable and not having an episode.
* Help the person avoid dangerous situations and behaviors, such as alcohol and drugs.
* Have realistic expectations for recovery.
* Offer unconditional love, no matter how hard it may be.

Caring for yourself:

* Do not let yourself get run down.
* Be prepared for early symptoms to turn into a crisis.
* Pay attention to your own physical and emotional well-being.
* Educate yourself.
* Find a support group.
* Get yourself in counseling.
* Keep a daily journal.

A few Lorisms (speaking from experience):

* Turn it over to God and never stop praying.
* Never give up.
* Follow your heart and not your head. God works through your heart.
* If you are trying to help a spouse of bipolar disorder, be supportive, pray for them, and be there for them however and whenever you are needed. It is not

helpful to continually point out the offenses of the bipolar person; it is not helpful to constantly remind them that their spouse needs help. They are well aware of all of that.

* Remember that they are living it every day. Support their decisions whether you agree with them or not.

* Be ready and willing to give unconditional love to the person suffering from the illness. They will need it when they come off their manic high or their depressive low. Be ready to forgive and move on.

Resources for help (these are only a few):
Depression and Bipolar Support Alliance
(800) 826-3632
www.dbsalliance.org

Freedom from Fear
(718) 351-1717
www.freedomfromfear.org

www.1on1health.com

National Mental Health Association
(800) 969-NMHA (6642)
www.nmha.org

Google or any other search engine

The best thing you can do to help yourself is pray. I didn't always remember this. Here are some verses to help you through tough times. These are only a few.

Afraid: Hebrews 13:5–6
Anxious: Psalm 46
Bitter/Critical: 1 Corinthians 13
Defeated: Romans 8:31–39
Depressed: Psalm 34
Discouraged: Psalm 23
Facing Crisis: Psalm 121
Lonely: Psalm 23
Needing Protection: Psalm 91
Weary: Matthew 11:28–30
Worried: 1 Peter 5:6–7
Courage: Psalm 27:14
Forgiveness: Mark 11:25–26
Hope: 1 Peter 1:13
Overcoming: John 16:33
Patience: Hebrews 10:36
Anger: Ephesians 4:26–27

Acknowledgments

Ask God for help daily. He is with you. You don't have to do it alone. You can't do it alone.

I have so many people that I need to thank for getting our family through the last four years.

To the love of my life, Donnie, thank you. Your encouragement to move forward with this book, knowing the humiliation it might bring you is selfless. Thank you for getting help and staying on your medication. When you see doubt creep into my mind, you give me gentle assurance that it wasn't you, that you are back now. You are an overcomer and will always be my hero.

To Taylor, Kaylee, and Lexi, thank you for not giving up on your parents. Thank you for sticking together and being strong. Thank you for forgiving the horrible things that you were put through. You are truly one of the greatest gifts in my life.

To my family, thank you. My mom was there for me whenever I needed her. My brother dropped everything to come when I needed him too. I know the rest of my family would have done anything I asked them too. And thank you, Dad, I felt your presence with me many times when I felt I couldn't go on one more day.

Julio, thank you for teaching me how to love unconditionally.

Tammy, thank you. You truly have become a sister to me during this time. I know you love your brother dearly, so thank you for believing me when others didn't. Thank you for your willingness to do whatever it took to help me protect Lexi. I know you sacrificed greatly.

Kadin and Krista, thank you. You let Donnie live with you for a couple of years and great healing took place at that time. Thank you for always listening and helping where you could. I always felt you understood and didn't judge.

To my dearest friend Lisa, thank you. Your e-mails, texts, and encouragement helped me get through these horrible times. Your unconditional love for my family is a treasured gift.

Thank you, Pastor Doug and Lesleigh. Hours of sitting and listening, refereeing, and your prayers were all appreciated. All the times you came in to check on Donnie so that I could continue work, all of your offers to take Lexi whenever I needed you too were a great help.

Doyle and Tasha, you were there for me and my girls no matter what we needed. Countless times, Doyle came running to help me with something that was broken at the house. Tasha listened for hours on end and organized a prayer meeting for us. You are appreciated.

Tommy and Beth, what great examples of friendship you have shown. The hours you spent helping me at the house, trying to talk sense into Donnie, everything you did was greatly appreciated. I knew I could call you day or night and you would come running. Thank you.

Josh, I couldn't have made it through our first episode without you. God definitely brought you to our family. Not to mention, the cows would have probably died without your help!

Chad and Carma, thank you for taking time out of your busy schedules to counsel us. I know, without a doubt, that you still pray for us. I believe you had a great part in Donnie's healing.

Denny and Erma, I cannot name everything you have done for our family. I remember Erma giving me a devotional book, maybe in December, before this all started again. I thought it strange as I didn't feel I really knew you that well. I guess God knew that I would come to heavily rely on that book and your friendship. God crossed our paths, I'm sure, because he knew you would be very instrumental in helping us through things. Everything Denny helped with at the house, all the times he stopped by to check on me and the girls, all the phone calls he gave Donnie cannot be repaid. Erma, thank you, you still touch base with me often to see how things are going and let me know you are still praying for us. You have become dear and treasured friends.

Rochelle, thank you for editing my book. Your encouragement was very needed and appreciated. You and Ron helped us through the first time, and I know if you would have been closer, you would have been more involved this time. In case you didn't know, you were one of my safe places for Lexi! I knew I could ask and not be turned away.

Thank you to the Living Center for helping me get my focus back on God.

A big thanks goes to the Christian Motorcycle Association. You saved my life. Praying without ceasing, though the night and across the nation, words cannot express my gratitude. I want to share that several months after we saw the CMA group in the rest area, I was driving through our small town and saw a few of the members. I recognized my friend Randy Kay, the one who lives close to me and so I decided to stop. I had visited Randy Kay at her work several times and updated her so I knew she would recognize me. However, before she saw me, one of the men riding along noticed me walking toward them. He said, "Is that Lori from the rest area last summer?" I was floored and couldn't believe he remembered me. I gave him an update and he told me then that Donnie and I are still prayed for at their monthly meetings and he would have a special update to share at the next meeting.

Randy Kay, I cannot tell you what your hugs mean to me every time I see you.

Tom, thank you. As soon as you realized something was off, you called to check on things often and tried several times to get through to Donnie. It might not seem like a big deal to you, but it was a big deal to me.

Dawn, I have not forgotten the countless times that you stopped by, often in tears for our family, during Donnie's first episode. Your care and concern touched my heart and was much appreciated.

And finally, my greatest thanks goes to God. Thank you for bringing us through and protecting us along the way. Thank you for the growing season and even for the growing pains.

CPSIA information can be obtained at www.ICGtesting.com
Printed in the USA
LVOW04s0313040815

448749LV00028B/453/P